DEDICATED TO

my dear students and to all "my girls"

past and present, on and off the ice

&

to my beautiful li'l sis, Nadia.

GODLY AND GIRLY

YOUR LIFE *in a Crazy, Messy, Confusing World*

LACY G. MARSH

CONCORDIA PUBLISHING HOUSE · SAINT LOUIS

Published by Concordia Publishing House
3558 S. Jefferson Avenue, St. Louis, MO 63118-3968
1-800-325-3040 • www.cph.org

Text © 2014 Lacy G. Marsh

Cover images: © iStockphoto.com

Illustrations: © iStockphoto.com; and iStock/Thinkstock

Manufactured in the United States of America

1 2 3 4 5 6 7 8 9 10   23 22 21 20 19 18 17 16 15 14

TABLE OF CONTENTS

Introduction

I pulled one lace tight and asked myself, *What am I doing?* My body hurt and my head was spinning with a light faintness that I dared not tell anyone about. This is what I want—what I was made to do. *This is my dream.* So why did it take every ounce of mental and physical strength I had to get out there on the ice?

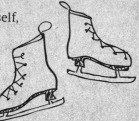

What am I doing? echoed against the walls of my brain. I pushed the words away and pulled the last lace through my fingers.

"Your body is a temple." I had heard that before. I had said that before. In fact, I'm sure I had quoted the verse to my friends. But when I looked at my temple—at my body—I saw what my coaches saw. I didn't measure up. They made it clear: either I look the part or walk away.

What is wrong with me? I often wondered. I hadn't given much thought to my physical flaws until the sharp finger of my coaches had pointed them out. I was a few months past eighteen that day as I looked at the reflection in the hockey rink glass and wondered how I'd ever be what I wanted to be, what they said I had to be. *I can do it,* I told myself. I had come this far from a cow-barn-turned-ice rink in western Montana by using every ounce of my will to succeed; I was sure I could manage this too.

·

Mirrors are funny. Televisions and magazines are even funnier. (And let's not even talk about images on the Internet!) Everyone we see—except the girl in the mirror—is perfect. Well, if not perfect, then they're unique, in a uniquely thin, sexy, model-ish way. I didn't think that I ever would buy into that whole fake, plastic surgery-look thing. I'm from rural Montana after all. But I *did* buy into it, and I paid a heavy price for it. Somewhere between the Rocky Mountains of the Bitterroot Valley, the traffic-congested highways of L.A., and the ski slopes of Idaho, I let the message seep in. This girl, who had stood for what she believed in, suddenly found herself believing she had to look a certain way to be worth something.

•

It was a logical conclusion, actually. My coaches didn't value me as highly when I gained a few pounds. The faces around the rink didn't smile in approval when my thighs grew wider. And that day, my reflection in the glass showed only a worthless outline of a wanna-be. I knew that I had to do something about this.

And so I did.

The image I desired was on my mind every minute of every day. I tried not to think about it—but it was beyond my control. I grew obsessed. And with every thought, a tightness rose in my chest. I felt panicked. I needed to fix this *now*. The results had to come soon; my identity, my very existence hinged on it.

I knew it was wrong to resort to eating-disorder-like behavior. *After all, I am still doing this for God,* I thought. I wanted to be the best ice dancer in the world for my Lord. Nothing less would satisfy me. I had shut out every other possible career path and zeroed in on this one mission for my life. I *would* get there. Imagine the impact I could have as an Olympic figure skater! "O Lord, I want to be the best in the world!" I often prayed as I pushed my blades across the white ice every day. Yes, I was doing this for God, and therefore I would do it the right way—I would not make myself throw up to lose weight.

•

She stood outside her house. She was gorgeous and tiny—half my size—and near my own age. She was *somebody*. And she made me realize that I was very fortunate to have someone like her working with me. She was my coach, my mentor, my friend. Coming off the international competitive track only years before, she was the perfect image of a successful ice dancer. And now, with a stack of glossy magazines in her arms, she challenged me: "You have to change your mind about a lot of things, Lacy. Like sex. And fashion. You are too much of a 'good girl.'" With that, she flopped the pile of flawless and seductive cover girls into my arms.

I got it. The message was clear. I had been hearing it for months: "You have to be *like this* to make it."

The message was clear on and off the ice. Every time I was in the ballet studio with my coach, I was shamed and verbally reminded of my failure. "A few more pounds," she'd advise as she compared my figure to her own. Soon she was giving me her old "fashionable" clothes too.

So now it was not only a number on the scale, but also the image of beauty and fashion trends that I needed to reflect. I was angry that she had told me such things. I believed I could handle the weight issue. I was doing fine—counting my calories, keeping a food diary, chewing gum when I wanted to eat. But this whole thing about not being a "good girl". . . . I wouldn't change my mind about morality and modesty and sex outside of marriage.

Besides losing weight, I was told that I had to change what I did *off* the ice in order to make it in the skating world. I was encouraged to "go out," stop playing Christian music during my practice sessions, and act more like people my age. But all the people my age were spending their nights drinking and crawling out of bedroom windows at odd hours of the morning. I wasn't naïve; I knew very well what they wanted me to be—and I couldn't be that person. So I was determined to adhere only to their demand that I lose weight.

There were days when I couldn't focus. When I wasn't skating, I worked full time at the rink, cleaning the building or doing bookwork. As I stared at the pages in front of me or grasped the mop, I felt like every ounce of strength had been drained from my body. I was weak. It didn't seem worth it to starve myself like this, but what option did I have?

I don't have an eating disorder, I told myself. I ate super-healthy, low-fat foods and worked out every day. I was doing this the right way. When I stopped having my monthly period, I knew I had lost a good percentage of body fat and I rejoiced in not having to deal with PMS. But my body wasn't rejoicing at all.

I have never been as physically tired as I was then. That was bad enough. But it was the emotional and mental fatigue that would leave a horrid impression on my mind for years to come. The cycle never stopped: the worry, the tightness, the panic. I'd lose the weight and somehow gain it back. Then I'd lose it again. I was never not on a diet.

■

I remember the day like it was yesterday. I even remember what I was wearing (gray sweatpants with a pink stripe down the legs and a Montana sweatshirt, in case you were wondering). I don't remember much of my skating lesson that morning; I'm not sure what we worked on. But I will never forget what my coach said to me as we walked away from the rink:

"You will never find a skating partner because of the way you look."

The horror of the last eight months went through my mind—the nightmare inside my head that had become so familiar to me; the way my body ached with weakness and frailty; the mornings I spent with an upset stomach due to my worrying; the condemning looks when I put a piece of food to my mouth.

The next thing I remember was calling my mom.

■

I didn't want to acknowledge that I had a problem. But underneath, I really did know that there was a lot wrong with the way I was treating my body, my mind, and my heart. I wanted to believe that I was serving God with my skating, but the truth was that my body image had become my idol. It consumed every waking moment and determined my mood every day. Of course I'd pray about it, but I was dead set on looking perfect so I could get an ice-dancing partner and climb the competitive ranks.

And that was only the half of it—in the ensuing years of professional show skating, the accompanying issues of being a good girl would take center stage, with the constant pressure to dress and skate in seductive ways. (More on this later!)

I'm twenty-four now . . . and healthy. A funny thing happened: when I finally stopped dieting and stopped listening to the world's messages, my body healed, my heart healed, and I was led to a new and fulfilling life. When I think about those years, especially that first year of training and living on my own, I feel a strange sense of gratitude. I don't know how I ever broke free of that cycle of self-destruction. Actually, I do know—it was by the grace of a God who loves me and a family that spoke truth to me when no one else did.

■

The pervasive message to conform to what the world told me I should be created the most trying times of my life. That message remains all around us. It may be difficult to recognize the message that our popular culture sends us. It may not be as obvious as what my coaches said to me, but the world and our culture shout out from all sides and whisper right next to us. Sometimes we don't hear the messages because we've grown up inside of them and to us they sound normal! Think about the movies, music, television programs, advertising, celebrities, and role models of today. All of these things and people portray to us how the typical girl behaves, talks, and thinks—*they create an **image** of what a girl or woman is.*

But what if much of what we believe about ourselves, who we should be, what our lives should be, our purpose on earth, and our relationships is false? What if God's message to us is starkly different from the one we thought was true?

■

I'm a coach now too. And I recognize the impact of cultural messages on my girls' faces because I've been there! They struggle with the same struggles I was confronted with—*am* confronted with. I tell them, and I'll tell you: You don't have to be "like that" to make it. You don't have to be "like that" to be worth something. You don't have to be "like that" to be happy. There is freedom and peace and healing in the message of God, and He wants you to hear it and believe it with every ounce of your being.

If you've experienced some of the things I went through or you've seen others go through them, if your heart has ached for something or you've wondered why you long, hurt, and dream in this crazy, messy (and rather confusing) world, then walk with me as we witness how this God of ours speaks a message that will change everything.

Neon Signs
and Flashing Arrows

CHAPTER ONE

"Be like This"

Who Are You?

Seems like a strange question, doesn't it? But hasn't it bounced around in your brain like a Ping-Pong ball? Although it appears to be a simple and obvious question, the answer can be the most unknown thing of all.

Who are you?

When we're born, we are given a name and a Social Security number. These attributes and a few others are recorded on official documents and are delivered to our parents or guardians. These pieces of paper serve as documents stating who we are. They identify us. But you could stare long and hard at them and never figure out who you *really* are. (You could also try closing your eyes, chanting some special words, and looking deep inside yourself . . . and see nothing.) Contrary to popular belief, we can't figure out who we are on our own. *We need an outside source to tell us who we are.*

I think we all know that, whether or not we consciously think about it. As humans, and especially as girls, we are constantly seeking something or someone that can clearly deliver the answer we crave. You may not be walking around your school or the mall or downtown with a clipboard and questionnaire asking "PLEASE, CAN YOU TELL ME WHO I AM?" in big bold letters, but you probably have asked yourself a few of these questions:

- What makes me important?
- Who out there is like me?
- What can I change about myself so I'm more like others?
- Does anyone think I'm pretty?
- How do I know how I'm supposed to feel or what I'm supposed to do?
- When will I be complete?
- Will anyone ever want me?

As girls, we yearn to be accepted, and we desperately want to fit in this busy and crazy world . . . so we look for answers. And we don't have to look far because there is a constant stream of messages flowing our way from every direction. It's as if the world is shouting at us with bright neon signs and flashing arrows, "All right, girl, you wanna know who you should be? Step right up and let me show you!! Be like **this** . . ."

This constant barrage of worldly messages answers all of our questions.

Or so it seems.

•

Maybe you are like me and didn't notice that there was a lot wrong with you until someone (un)kindly pointed it out to you. Or perhaps you woke up one day and suddenly saw for yourself that you didn't fit the mold of perfection. Maybe you have always felt second-rate.

Regardless of how you arrived at this place, the world is ready to help transform you into a different you. But what the world—with its neon lights, flashy arrows, and constant messages—doesn't tell you is that its answers are all lies.

Be like This: Body Image

I've long been in the habit of writing out my prayers to God. I have stacks and stacks of journals—most are colorful spiral-bound notebooks—filled with page after page of longhand. Occasionally, I pick up an old notebook and flip through it. If you were to look at the entries of my teen and young adult years, you'd find that among these pages of prayers are scattered skating notes and food diaries—the fabric of my life. My struggle would be present on the pages, apparent with every word.

Sunday, October, 27, 2007

Many things weigh my heart this night; one is eating away at me—and Lord, how it hurts. A problem I've tried to push away, tried to reason, tried to give to You, but it comes and nags at me until I'm emotionally exhausted. To some it must seem so silly— but to me it engulfs me and is so horribly real. It's so pressing;

I feel it wants to crush me. And Lord, I don't know how to deal with it.

My weight, Lord, my "look"—the "look."

Could my coach be right in saying no one will skate with me because of how I look? No. But then, why does all this haunt me? Everyone is telling me that to fit in with competitive ice dancers I must be thinner . . . achieve the "look." I must lose "mass."

Then there are the questions. Do I fight against it and break the mold? Do I just lose a little? Do I go all out? Can my body handle that?

Why must my image be defined by how big my butt is or how thick my thighs are? Will people look at me on the ice and see talent and Your gift, or will they merely see potential if "she slims down"? Am I the only dancer who exists that looks like me? Will anyone accept me?

I feel brainwashed, Lord. The media, the coaches, the people all around. How come I can't look at any girl without comparing my body to hers? How come I feel I must stare the mirror down until I see thinness? How come I despise my own self?

There's an image in my mind and I think I'll only be a good skater if I look like that perfect, flawless image. Lord, I'm a perfectionist, but I'm having a hard time finding perfection in me.

It didn't stop there. Years after I left competitive and show skating, the struggle clung to me. Even now it comes and plays havoc on my mind, and I wonder if my worth will change with every number on the bathroom scale. Although I don't look to coaches anymore, I find myself looking to others for validation about how my body looks and if I'm desirable. If I find out a guy thinks I look good—then wow, am I a happy camper! But if I feel ugly, or my curly hair has a little more frizz than curl, or if I just feel heavier that day—then I can barely hold in my fear, and that cycle of hating myself comes knocking on my door.

•

I had been told there was a specific formula for beauty. Look "like this": cut your hair this length, wear this style of makeup, and (most of all) be thin. If I had one hair misplaced or one extra pound, I felt like I had failed and couldn't be beautiful.

I based my worth as a skater on the formula. I based my attractiveness as a girl on the formula. I based my value as a person on the formula.

Every aspect of my life was about following the blueprint for beauty. And everything around me said something about that blueprint. It was endless. I feared what would happen if I fell short: I'd never find a skating partner; I'd never have a boyfriend. I wanted to believe that somehow I could be accepted, wanted, and valued—but the image of failure in the mirror wouldn't let me.

•

Where are you right now? Have you been to the same places of depression and fear? While you may not have grown up in a highly appearance-focused sport or art, you have undoubtedly heard what your "coaches"— popular TV, music, and other media— have been telling you. You've seen what the world considers perfect and beautiful. They've delivered a mold of the "flawless you" to your doorstep, and you wonder how you'll ever fit. And when you consider the things you could do to make yourself fit the mold, your stomach turns.

So, what do you do? How can you wake up from the nightmare?

Well, you can try to transform yourself into perfection. That's what I tried to do. But the more I tried, the harder I worked, the further out of my reach perfection became. Eventually, the only thing I reached was a weakened body and a nonexistent self-worth.

What I learned through it all is that the key isn't in trying hard enough—it's in surrender. This might surprise you, but it isn't your battle. It's God's.

"But it's my body," you say? Yes, true. But God is your Creator, your Potter, your Artist who crafted every stitch of that body . . . as well as that heart inside of you. When you choose to abuse either in order to somehow transform yourself, you will fail.

Victory is found in an unusual place. It isn't found in endless diets, excessive exercise, starvation, new clothes, or anything else you might try. It's found at Jesus' feet. At the foot of the cross. There in the dirty mud mixed with the blood of a Savior hanging above you. He didn't go through all that agony so you could endure the relentless agony of trying to make yourself beautiful according to the world's standard. Jesus confirmed your beauty right there on that cross. He won the battle for your body right then. Victory isn't pending—it's a done deal, a sure thing. Don't misunderstand; I'm not saying He won the victory to make you a size 2. I'm saying He has already defeated the hell of eating disorders and hating our bodies. He defeated the *need* to be a size 2. He defeated our doubts of inadequacy and the lies we've been believing.

■

Sounds great, right?!

Okay, you may be thinking, *okay. But Jesus died a long time ago. What can His cross victory over all those things really do about MY struggle here and now?*

For starters, it cuts in on the formula for beauty. The cross puts a big ol' *X* right through the world's blueprint. It cancels it out; it reduces it to nothing. Instead of neon signs saying "Be like this!" the cross says, "Christ made you like *this*."

It says, "This is what I—Christ—did, so you don't have to."

It says, "I am so captivated by **you** that I had to save you."

Does that give you a different perspective of yourself? Do you see yourself differently when you sit at the feet of your Savior and look through His eyes? Can you see what He sacrificed His very life to save?

 You.

THE WIN

Christ's victory over sin and death was a victory over the sin of abusing your body and the death of hating yourself. It was a conquest over seeing yourself as worthless and ugly. It was a rescue from struggling on your own to fit into some cultural mold. It was a real victory at a real place on a real day that came to you in the real water and Word of your Baptism. You were baptized into this very victory. The battle has already been won for you, the outcome decided. Christ's triumph is *your* triumph!

So every time the world tries to blind you with its flashing signs and neon arrows, turn your eyes to a different message. A message of victory credited to your account. A message of a cross and a Savior who thinks you are precious enough to die for.

He called you and paid the price for you even when you were stained in the repulsiveness of sin! Think about that—He must truly cherish you!

Most of all, remember God's message that it isn't about what you or I *do,* but about what already *has been done for us.* Stop striving for your own perfection and see it instead in the face of the risen Jesus standing at your side.

> And you, who were dead in your trespasses and the uncircumcision of your flesh, God made alive together with Him, having forgiven us all our trespasses, by canceling the record of debt that stood against us with its legal demands. This He set aside, nailing it to the cross. He disarmed the rulers and authorities

and put them to open shame, by triumphing over them in Him.
(Colossians 2:13–15)

DIVE INTO THE VICTORY!

First, pour out your heart to God in a letter. Tell Him about whatever is consuming you. Believe me, He won't fail to hear you—He *delights* in listening to you!

Dearest Lord God,

FROM HIS LIPS

Now it's your time to hear Him . . . to listen. Open your Bible and see what He says to you about all this.

If you don't know where to start, look at these messages of truth God has already said about how He sees you and your body. I'll let these verses speak for themselves!

You are altogether beautiful, my love;
there is no flaw in you.
(Song of Solomon 4:7)

.

For You formed my inward parts;
    You knitted me together in my mother's womb.
I praise You, for I am fearfully and wonderfully made.
Wonderful are Your works;
    my soul knows it very well.
My frame was not hidden from You,
when I was being made in secret,
    intricately woven in the depths of the earth.
Your eyes saw my unformed substance.
(Psalm 139:13–16a)

.

Behold, you are beautiful, my love;
    behold, you are beautiful;
    your eyes are doves.
(Song of Solomon 1:15)

Pocket It

Write out the following verses on a piece of paper and slide it into your pocket each day when you get dressed. When you have a spare moment, reach for the paper instead of reaching for a magazine or cell phone. (When I was in school, I read mine during lunch break.) God's truth and power will become mighty inside of you as His beautiful message takes root!

Week 1:

- Psalm 44:3
- Galatians 2:20
- Isaiah 26:12
- Colossians 2:13–15

Week 2:

- Romans 8:37
- Romans 6:3
- 2 Corinthians 12:7–12
- 1 Corinthians 15:42–44

Be like This: Character

In the professional ice show I skated in, there were two especially gorgeous and well-liked girls in their mid-twenties. These two girls were kind to me. As a younger skater, I had always been looked upon as the girl who had potential, but I certainly wasn't one of *them*. While I didn't admire everything about their lives, I admired that they treated me well.

One day they took me under their wings and gave me some advice about how to be more confident. As we stood near the railing on the ice, they made suggestions about my clothing style and attitude. They said that if I wore little booty-shorts and skated like I knew I was hot, then I'd catch everyone's attention. Perhaps I'd even get that elusive skating partner I had been searching for.

What they said made sense at the time: one way to counteract my low self-esteem and body image was to change outward things about my character and personality. If I would dress and act like them, then not only would I feel better about my body (because I would have *waaayyy* more attention, regardless of the extra few pounds), but I would be making a name for myself in the skating world as well. The two things I wanted!

For a while it put a little pep in my step to think that these two girls believed I could have what it takes if only I altered a few little things about myself. I let some of their suggestions seep in. They weren't saying I had to throw away my morals, just that I shouldn't be so strict about them. They didn't say I was worthless as I was; they just thought I'd be better if I changed.

So I compromised. Sure, I shimmied to the show music and wore revealing costumes, but I didn't sleep around or anything. And sure, I tried to be sexually appealing to fit in, but it wasn't like I had thrown away my faith or my desire to be a faithful wife someday.

What I failed to see was that my actions—even the small superficial ones—*portrayed to the world who I was and what I cherished.* I couldn't be sure that people who watched me in the show were seeing that I cherished purity, morals, and my relationship with God above all else. My actions were a giant billboard pointing only to me—and in all the wrong ways. I was trying desperately to promote myself. I wanted to make it, to fit in, to be somebody. And I reasoned that a little compromise here and there wouldn't hurt anything. In fact, maybe it would make me confident about *who* I was. Maybe it would give me an identity.

> **Character**—it's the stuff that makes up your personality, the traits of who you are revealed *in* your actions, words, and thoughts.

Ironically, altering myself to fit in the world's mold of character didn't bring me an identity. It brought me the exact opposite. It was as if I had two personalities that were in constant conflict. There was the girl who loved her God and desired to please Him and the girl whose actions said she loved the world and desired to fit into it. It made me feel so divided. And the worst part was that it seemed my actions were actually turning me into someone I didn't really want to be. Everything in my world was making it seem like I didn't have a choice. But did I?

SINFUL NATURE MAKEOVER

Are you cringing as you think of your own actions, words, and thoughts? I certainly am! Let's face it: if every thought of ours were revealed, we'd be horrified. If every word said in anger were published, we'd hide in our bedrooms for all eternity. And if every secret action were recorded and played back to our families, we'd be ashamed forever.

The bad stuff—the not-so-pure thoughts, the less-than-honorable deeds, the yuck within us—it all marks us as sinful and unclean. This is the character of our "old self," our sinful nature.

We were born into this corrupted nature. Ever since that fateful moment in the Garden of Eden when Adam and Eve disobeyed God, every human has been stained with sin. And the consequences of that sin are devastating—eternal separation from God and eternal damnation. To top it all off, because of this sinful nature, we can do nothing to please our Lord! We're too dirty for Him to even consider our good deeds as good.

But there is good news—the Good News. The cross and empty tomb of Christ changed all that. Just as Christ has won the battle over the bonds of hating yourself and your body, He has won rescue from the sinful nature that enslaves you.

> [You,] having been set free from sin, have become slaves of righteousness. (Romans 6:18)

On our own, we can't even hope to produce a character of good fruit that pleases God. We are so incredibly corrupted by the sinful nature living inside of us. But again, the cross marks a big ol' *X* right through what would otherwise keep us from Him. Christ forever broke the chains of our slavery. And the consequence of that is glorious! We no longer have an obligation to obey the old sinful nature; we are set free to obey God in a character of righteousness.

We went from being unable to do one single thing that would be pleasing to God to having complete freedom to do so! And complete power within us to do so!

And it's all because of the Holy Spirit.

You see, the Holy Spirit has taken up residence in your heart. He moved in the moment you believed or were baptized. Why does that matter? Well, because He doesn't just sit back and leave the décor of your heart as it is. He is a meticulous interior designer—**and He's changing the interior of you.** No longer will decorations of selfishness, immodesty, and envy fill the cabinets of your heart-home. The wallpaper of pride must go too. Not to mention the peeling paint of hatred and unforgiveness. The Holy Spirit is making the place brand-new. His goal: remove every ounce of your old sinful nature and make your heart gorgeous with the attributes of Christ. He gives us the power to say no to a character of sin and yes to a character of Christ.

An Alternative Offer

"Hold on!" the world shouts. "I have an alternative offer! What if I told you that you could act one way and still *be* another?"

The rival interior designer—the world—has many alternative decorations and furnishings of character on display. (You guessed it: bright neon lights and flashing arrows!) And their sales pitch is appealing: keep your faith, but act however you want. The bonus—you fit in with the crowd!

Can't you hear the relentless ads:

"Put *this* in your heart-home!"

"*This* is the latest fashion!"

"Wanna be someone? Just do *this!*"

"Forget the vintage Holy Spirit—redecorate your character your own way! It's character feng shui!"

I listened to my ice-show peers and coaches just as if I were listening to a commercial. They were pitching their product and I was buying. I didn't understand at first that I really was considering their offer. But I was, and it came through one little compromise at a time.

My coaches were constantly bringing to my attention that I was too much of a "good girl." They didn't want my relationship with God to reflect in my image as an ice dancer. Faith was fine as long as it didn't interfere with getting a partner or hanging out with the right crowd or skating to the sexy show numbers. They simply wanted me to leave my faith at church for Sunday mornings. *"Separate your faith from your actions"* was their message.

In that context, it made sense, just as starving myself had seemed to make sense. All I needed to do to get where I wanted to go was compromise a little. But eventually I understood that even one little compromise was all the devil and the world needed, one little toehold that eventually became a full grip on my heart.

The conflict between having the Holy Spirit interior-heart-designer living in me while at the same time the world was pounding at my mind made me wonder: can a person separate her relationship with Jesus from her actions?

Can we act one way and truly be another?

The question reached a pinnacle during my last season in the ice show. The new choreography, music, and costumes made a statement, but it wasn't the statement I wanted to make. I knew that if I performed the numbers, I'd be giving the little girls who looked up to me the same message my coach had handed me along with all those pop magazines several years before: "You have to be like this if you want to make it." And I would be buying into the world's two-faced lie—your actions don't make you who you are.

Could I really have skated to music with lyrics that made sex outside of marriage sound glorious, danced in sensual ways, worn skimpy costumes on the ice—and still proclaim that I cherish purity and godliness? No way! My actions would have screamed a message so loud that no cross around my neck or purity ring on my finger could out-shout.

James said, "Show me your faith apart from your works, and I will show you my faith by my works" (James 2:18b). It was about time I did that.

So . . . I left.

> "What will it profit a man if he gains the whole world and forfeits his soul?"—Jesus (Matthew 16:26a)

I could have gained the world. The world of skating fame—my lifelong dream—could have been mine. And the cost? Perhaps my very soul. That's a hefty price to pay for a counterfeit life. You see, if you look closely enough, you will discover that what the world is selling isn't all diamonds and gold. No, the world's bling and sparkles are just counterfeits and phony substitutes.

Counterfeits don't satisfy. Sure, I could have climbed my way to the top and gotten a spot as a principal skater in a show someday, but for what? I would have become a person I didn't want to be. I would have portrayed an image to everyone around me that I wouldn't have been proud of and my God certainly wouldn't have been proud of. I would have lost my true identity, pushed away the Holy Spirit, and missed the amazing life He is giving me now. I would have gained the counterfeit world and lost my soul.

THE CHOICE

Sit back down in that muddy spot at the foot of the cross and look up. Can you see it? The old you—all your pride, vanity, selfishness, hatred, envy, lust, self-promotion—nailed to the crossbeam. The ugliness of your old sinful nature hangs still and lifeless from the cross within Christ's body. He bore it for you. He took it from you, put it on Himself, and let it be killed even as He was killed.

The giant billboard now shows Jesus. "Look!" He says. "I destroyed the power of sin. It doesn't have to control you anymore. I give you a new heart and a new life that satisfies!"

When you look up at your Savior, do you want to take back those sinful attributes He died for? When you look up at that dying Savior, do you wish to be like Him? Well, that's exactly what the cross accomplishes—His death on the cross gives you the ability to be like Him in your thoughts, words, actions, and desires.

You no longer have to be a slave to sin. Just look at the immense power within you. That power is God Himself, fighting the old nature for you and giving you the tools you need to resist it—His Word, His body and blood, and Baptism. No longer a slave to sin, you have new life. This new life has brought you new character—His character. He has resurrected *His* image within you. You bear His likeness of character. And that zealous interior designer, the Holy Spirit, is continuously transforming you into the similarity of Christ.

> Now the Lord is the Spirit, and where the Spirit of the Lord is, there is freedom. And we all, with unveiled face, beholding the glory of the Lord, **are being transformed into the same image from one degree of glory to another. For this** comes from the Lord who is the Spirit. (2 Corinthians 3:17–18; emphasis mine)

If we choose again to be a slave to the old nature, soon we will become that nature. We cannot act one way and be another on the inside. If we continually behave one way, we will certainly become that way.

Don't let your actions, thoughts, and words mold you into someone you don't want to be. When you feel it happening, sit back down at the cross. Ponder the mighty Spirit that your loving Savior sent to you. And ask God to daily overcome the old character within you. The power of God inside of you is ever so much stronger than the power of the world outside of you.

> His divine power has granted to us all things that pertain to life and godliness, through the knowledge of Him who called us to His own glory and excellence. (2 Peter 1:3)

> ■

> So you also must consider yourselves dead to sin and alive to God in Christ Jesus.

> Let not sin therefore reign in your mortal body, to make you obey its passions. Do not present your members to sin as instruments for unrighteousness, but present yourselves to God as those who have been brought from death to life, and your member to God as instruments for righteousness. For sin will have no dominion over you, since you are not under law but under grace. (Romans 6:11–14)

CHARACTER CHECK

✿ What are the bright neon signs and flashing arrows telling you about the image of the "typical" girl? What do they say about how you should act, dress, and *be* like?

✿ Can you identify the subtle and not-so-subtle messages the world sends to you in your everyday life? (Being able to identify them will help guard you from falling prey to their catchy sales pitches.)

✿ When people talk about character, you may hear them quote this line: "Be true to yourself." Is that a good motto to live by? Why or why not?

✿ Explore what that means in light of the following passages:

- 1 John 3:1
- 1 Peter 2:9–10
- 1 Peter 1:23

✿ Can you see the two contrasting types of character in Galatians 5:16–26?

✿ Now read 1 Peter 3:3–6. What does God say a character of beauty looks like within a godly girl?

✿ When you wonder if your character is "Christlike," ask yourself this: Do my actions match what God says is true?

✿ Where can we find what is absolutely **true?**

✿ Right on! His Word. Let us daily, then, get familiar with it so that we can resist the two-faced message of the worldly interior designer and follow the example of a character of truth that Christ has purchased for us!

POCKET IT

You know the drill. :)

Week 3:

- 1 Peter 1:13–16
- 1 Corinthians 10:13
- 1 Corinthians 10:31
- John 14:20–21

CHAPTER TWO

What Happened to My Fairy Tale?

Think about the ideal list of the major accomplishments you plan for your life. What would you include?

1.

2.

3.

4.

5.

6.

LIFE. Four little letters spell the concept that includes everything we do and everything we hope to do. Have you thought much about your life? You may not have because there is much around us that tells us what it is all about (and I'm not just talking the Hokey Pokey). But maybe you have given it a lot of thought.

If you're like me, your ideal life follows a neat little order—something like this:

- Birth (Look how cute I am!!)
- Childhood
- Surviving high school
- College (in my case, the University of Slippery Ice)
- Career
- Finding that perfect someone and falling in love (*XOXO*)
- Marrying that perfect someone
- Buying the house down the street (the one with the bay window)
- Starting a family

And that's usually where I stop because that pretty much sums up life—you have it all there: education, true love, home, and little tikes in diapers. True, not everyone has the same list. But for the most part, we all know how it goes—we grow up, become successful, find Mr. Right, and the rest is glorious!

An ex-boyfriend put it to me like this (as we were breaking up): "Life is about two things: one, finding that perfect someone, and two, having lots of good stories to tell in heaven." Apparently, I wasn't that perfect someone, and I wouldn't be telling this story on the other side of the pearly gates.

Take a moment with me and let's think about our favorite movies—especially chick flicks. How does the sequence go? Extremely romantic and attractive boy gets bright and wonderful girl, boy disastrously loses girl, boy and girl stumble around like lost souls, boy miraculously gets girl back, everything in boy's and girl's life falls beautifully in place, and they live happily ever after.

But what if real life isn't as neat and tidy as all that?

Are you there yet? I was in my twenties before I realized that my idea of the perfect little package of life wasn't going to be as perfect as I hoped. Things had happened. The wrapping paper was torn and the bow was all askew. And I felt like living a messed-up life was meaningless—if my life wasn't going to follow my fairy-tale story line, then I wasn't sure I wanted to live it.

You see, I had based my ideal life on two end-aims, two great goals:

1. Becoming an Olympic champion
2. Becoming a wife

They both fit perfectly on my list.

When the first one went unrealized, I felt like I had failed and lost who I was. So I put all my hope on the second one. Since I was no longer pursuing the Olympics, finding a husband would bring meaning to my life, and accomplishing that would fulfill me. And then I witnessed firsthand that marriages can shatter: my parents' marriage became like a nightmare scene from a horror movie. I felt incredibly disillusioned and began to wonder that if marriage could be so fragile, could there be any purpose left for my life or any possibility for happiness?

Are there no "happily ever afters"?

During those months, I struggled with the fact that goals can go unrealized. Which part about what I believed was wrong? The goodness of marriage? That I should use my talents to pursue a career? That I could believe in dreams or happy endings? That my life had purpose? I felt like the heart of living my life had died.

As I cried my way through the darkness, my God was right beside me. He didn't give up on me when I questioned everything I knew about—well, about everything. He didn't turn away when I sat in my anger and despair. Like the healer He is, God patiently and tenderly began to show me where I had been wrong. (And I was wrong about a lot.)

I was wrong in viewing life as a laundry list of to-dos to be checked off.

I was wrong in thinking that following a formula would bring me happiness.

I was wrong in taking my cues from the world instead of from what God says about the meaning of life.

I was wrong to believe that I had to wrap up my little fairy tale while I was still living on earth.

The Opening Chapters

Do you know that you already have your end goal? that your end-aim is guaranteed? that God has indeed written your story as a beautiful fairy tale and you're living in the **opening chapters** of your life story? We don't accomplish our "happily ever after" on this side of eternity. That chapter is written and waits in heaven.

The world would have us believe otherwise. Because the world tries to mislead us, we might envision heaven as a roomful of Christians singing lengthy hymns and twiddling their thumbs while God is a far-off glow in the clouds. We might picture heaven as some sparkling (but boring) castle in the sky. It's the place we go after we're finished living.

But what if all of our living doesn't take place down here?

I had believed the **"only one life" lie.** It's the one that goes this way: "I'd better get all my living in today because there won't be any on the other side of eternity." Now, it wasn't some wild and crazy party type of living that I sought, but I did feel hurried and pressured to arrange a perfect story line before my life was over. Yet through my dark days, I realized that there were two problems with my thinking:

1. My story was no longer perfect, and
2. I was seeing only the *beginning* of the story.

What would a well-plotted book be without an interesting beginning and a good ending? If you think about it, a messy, disorganized, imperfect plot in the first couple of chapters makes for a great book! How boring it would be to reach the fairy-tale climax halfway through; there'd be no reason to keep reading to the end!

> I thought that losing my perfect fairy tale meant losing my reason for living. But in fact, losing my perfect fairy tale *gave me the reason* to keep on living the story.

Some conflict, despair, perseverance, and mystery before a neat and tidy ending is what keeps the reader engaged. God knew that our lives on earth would be full of trials and imperfect events (John 16:33); that's why He sent Someone, His Son, to overcome all of them and guarantee a happy ending for us in heaven.

We've been programmed by the world around us to base our lives on chapter ten when twenty-three is waiting down the road. Or up in the sky. If we live our ending down here on the ground, we are sure to find that it isn't all that we hoped for. Things will happen that break our hearts, infect our bodies, scar our families. But if we live knowing that in heaven all these sorrows and wrongs will be made right, we can withstand anything down here on earth—for those trials only disrupt the opening chapters. What freedom that gives! We don't have to hold so tightly. We can let go of the death-grips on our lists of life because death will bring us the rest of the story!

And the rest of the story—the best part of the story—is heaven. Remember the singing saints with twiddling thumbs? That isn't what heaven is like. Although we don't know a whole lot about life in heaven, we do know that it is the place where we will truly *live*. Forget our version of what it will be like; our human brain can't imagine the truth of eternity. God's Word tells us that heaven will be so incredibly glorious (and so far from boring) that we won't be able to stop praising Him for it!

God gives us a glimpse of this perfect place:

> "For behold, I will create new heavens
>   and a new earth,
> and the former things shall not be remembered
>   or come into mind.
> But be glad and rejoice forever
>   in that which I create;
> for behold, I create Jerusalem to be a joy,
>   and her people to be a gladness.
> I will rejoice in Jerusalem
>   and be glad in My people;
> no more shall be heard in it the sound of weeping
>   and the cry of distress. . . .
>
> They shall build houses and inhabit them;
>   they shall plant vineyards and eat their fruit.
> They shall not build and another inhabit;

they shall not plant and another eat;
for like the days of a tree shall the days of My people be,
    and My chosen shall long enjoy the work of their
    hands.
They shall not labor in vain
    or bear children for calamity,
for they shall be the offspring of the blessed of the LORD,
    and their descendants with them.
Before they call I will answer;
    while they are yet speaking I will hear.
The wolf and the lamb shall graze together;
    the lion shall eat straw like the ox,
    and dust shall be the serpent's food.
They shall not hurt or destroy
    in all My holy mountain,"
says the LORD.

Isaiah 65:17–19, 21–25

■

"Behold, the dwelling place of God is with man. He will dwell with them, and they will be His people, and God Himself will be with them as their God. He will wipe every tear from their eyes, and death shall be no more, neither shall there be mourning, nor crying, nor pain anymore, for the former things have passed away." Revelation 21:3 4

"The former things." Those broken lists of our lives—gone. In heaven we will be so far beyond happy that we won't be able to remember what sad was. Everything that doesn't make sense now will make sense then. And we'll see our purpose face-to-face, for we shall see God face-to-face. We'll see what we were created for—the last chapter, the happily ever after, life lived alongside God.

Could this change how we view everything now?
Could this give us new reason to live here on
earth? Would it make us see our end-aims and life
lists differently?

And What about Your Life?

What has interrupted your list, your story? Cancer? Divorce? The night you lost your virginity? The day disaster came? Depression? A broken heart?

Everyone's list is interrupted. Even if you are able to check off every to-do on your perfect list, your life will still be interrupted by feelings of dissatisfaction and emptiness.

The truth is that having our lists interrupted might be the greatest blessing we receive. That's because if we store up an ideal of what we think our lives should be, we become susceptible to having that ideal destroyed. Thieves of sin and sadness can break in and steal it. And then what are we left with? For me, I had nothing left because my heart was here on earth with my treasure, and my treasure had been taken.

> "Do not lay up for yourselves treasures on earth, where moth and rust destroy and where thieves break in and steal, but lay up for yourselves treasures in heaven, where neither moth nor rust destroys and where thieves do not break in and steal. For where your treasure is, there your heart will be also." —Jesus (Matthew 6:19–21)

Something incredible happens when your heart moves to heaven.

When your heart lives there, everything here is endurable. Everything here, including the yucky stuff, has purpose. Our hearts can take hold of that "happily ever after" even while we live out these opening chapters now.

But how can we do that? How can we relocate our hearts from this neighborhood of earth to heaven while we are still here? We get on the moving van of God's Word and let it transport our treasure to heaven, that's how!

The Holy Spirit uses the Holy Word of God to secure the location of your heart by revealing God to you. In that Word, you see that your heart belongs where He is, and heaven will be its new home. Continue to ask Him to keep your heart where your real life is—with Christ. The Author of your faith—God—will be ever so glad you asked, and the journey He takes you on will be better than any road trip you can imagine!

> If then you have been raised with Christ, seek the things that are above, where Christ is, seated at the right hand of God. Set your minds on things that are above, not on things that are on earth. For you have died, and your life is hidden with Christ in God. When Christ **who is your life** appears, then you also will appear with Him in glory. (Colossians 3:1–4; emphasis mine)

So What Is It All about Then?

If life isn't about our lists, if our fairy-tale ending awaits in heaven, **then what is this life on earth about?**

Great question!

While God has given each of us different talents, things to accomplish, and stories to live, He has also given everyone the same broader purpose. Jesus says it best:

"You shall love the Lord your God with all your heart and with all your soul and with all your mind. This is the great and first commandment. And a second is like it: You shall love your neighbor as yourself." (Matthew 22:37–39)

When your life centers around these two commandments, then your goals, dreams, talents, and skills can be used to "live for God." In all the things you do in your life, you can do them to *make God famous,* to be an effective helper to those around you, and to live out a proclamation of love for Him.

What are the first steps to living a life like this for God?

For me, it was accepting that my list of life wasn't going to bring me happiness.

Next, I had to let my heavenly Father move my heart to heaven through **surrender.**

"For whoever would save his life will lose it, but whoever loses his life for My sake will find it." —Jesus (Matthew 16:25)

"How can I possibly lose my life?" you ask. Well, think of it this way:

Losing your life is like saying, "Lord, I want whatever You want for my life. I know I've made plans and have goals and dreams, but I want my life to be about You in everything I do—no matter what that means. Show me what You want for me and I will do it with Your help, Lord."

It's saying, *"Here I am! Send me"* (Isaiah 6:8; emphasis mine), no matter where He positions the course of your life.

▪

I used to think that surrendering my dreams and plans to God meant losing who I was—losing my purpose.

Because I'm a Christian, I thought that I had based my life around "living for God." But eventually I recognized that I hadn't surrendered to Him at all; I still held ever so tightly to my own prescribed goals. The funny thing was, the tighter I held on to them, the more miserable I was. I felt myself being drained of motivation as I clung to what I thought would bring me identity, worth, and happiness. And all the while, I convinced myself that I was doing this for God.

I remember the day that burden was taken from my shoulders.

I sat by a little window overlooking a Pennsylvania suburb. I was there to train; I was skating in a facility with multiple rinks, multiple world champions, multiple Olympic coaches, and multiple days when I felt like I couldn't bear one more minute of it. This dream of mine was supposed to be my reason for living. It was supposed to fulfill me. But I felt emptier and more depressed than ever before. I reached for my phone.

"Mom?" I cried as she picked up. "Will you still love me if I never make it to the Olympics?"

My mom had never pushed me to make it to the Olympic level—in fact, *I* begged to go to the rink; I set the goal for myself. I knew my parents would love me and be proud of me no matter what I did, but I had made every part of my life about the Olympics, and now I needed a voice outside of my own head to tell me that my dream didn't define me. I needed to hear my mom tell me that I was going to be okay if I gave up. Not only did she do that, she told me that I'd be okay if I quit skating altogether, and that if I did, she wouldn't be disappointed in me. That blew my mind, actually. Somehow my mom saw my worth and purpose outside of who I was as a skater, when all I could see was myself as a failure.

I can't help crying as I write this. The impact of that moment in my life changed everything. It was at that moment that God began to open my eyes to who I was—*who I was* ***in Him***—and what my true purpose was on this earth.

■

Not every dream should be given up in the sense that you quit pursuing it. (Dreams and goals can be amazing gifts from the Lord that He wants you to pursue! We'll see that in a later chapter.) But every dream and life should be given *into* His hand to do whatever He will with it. If you aren't willing to place it in His palm, then it has replaced Him as "god" in your life. You won't be able to fully live out your purpose to love Him and love your neighbor. But surrendered inside His capable hands, your life can flourish! He can hold it for you so that you don't have to grasp it in fear of failing. Think of it like sand. If you clench it too tightly, it runs through your fingers and you're left holding air. But when you place your future, your desires, your skills, your every plan inside God's hands, He can make it more incredible than you ever imagined.

As a young girl, I never thought that I'd say this, but when I placed my life in God's hands, He replaced it with one that was even better!

> I have been crucified with Christ. It is no longer I who live, but Christ who lives in me. And the life I now live in the flesh I live by faith in the Son of God, who loved me and gave Himself for me. (Galatians 2:20)

SO, LET'S RECAP

If your ideal story is ruined, you *aren't* ruined. In fact, what can possibly ruin the story of a girl who is sought and won by the most amazing King and glorious Author?! If you don't believe me, look up Romans 8:28–39! And while your Bible is open, consider these passages too:

✿ Life isn't about our lists. Following a formula can't bring you happiness. I love Psalm 16:11.

✿ Ask God to move your treasure and your heart to heaven! You won't regret it! More faves: Psalm 27:8 and 1 Peter 1:3–9.

✿ Listen to what God says about "life" instead of taking your cues from the world. See 1 John 2:15–17.

✿ There's a happy ending coming—guaranteed—in heaven. Rejoice in your fairy tale! See Philippians 3:20–21.

✿ Don't believe the "only one life" lie! There will be much living in heaven—the greener grass ain't on this side of eternity, girl! See John 11:25–26.

✿ Place your life and dreams in God's hands and let Him make your life about Him! See 1 Corinthians 12:4–6.

✿ God has given us purpose and joy in this life on earth! See Psalm 4:6–7.

Talk to God about It

Dearest Lord God,

I've believed many misconceptions about life. Everything around me seems to tell me what life is all about—but now I want to hear what You say. Lord, I want my life to be about You. I want You to have the pen—You are the Author of my story. Help me to see the gift You've guaranteed me in heaven. Move my heart there so that I might live down here knowing You have a beautiful fairy-tale ending waiting for me with You. And fill me with Your purpose, Father, that all my talents and dreams might be used to love You and those around me. Whatever You want for my life—that is what I want too.

Lord, Your will (and best!) be done! I love You.

Amen.

Pocket It

Week 4:

- Psalm 16:11
- Psalm 27:8
- 1 Peter 1:3–9
- 1 John 2:15–17

Week 5:

- Philippians 3:20–21
- John 11:25–26
- 1 Corinthians 12:4–6
- Psalm 4:6–7

Living IN
God's Message

CHAPTER 3

Your Romance

As the bridegroom rejoices over the bride, so shall your God rejoice over you. (Isaiah 62:5b)

When you sit down to watch a romantic comedy, do you ever get that strange feeling? Maybe you thought you were the only one who experienced that sudden tightness rising in your chest. It's like your heart is . . . well, aching.

I feel it often. A pulling. As if I can suddenly feel the presence of my heart inside my body, stretching and yearning behind my ribs. Our livers don't usually ache, nor our brains, or spleens. But the heart . . . the heart is that strange organ that seems to do much more than pump blood. It pumps emotion, longing, pain, and joy.

Back to the romantic comedy. What causes that strange sensation within us? Perhaps the scene where the handsome single guy walks toward the girl we secretly wish we were? Or when he gently takes her hand in his for the first time? Or when he defies all odds to prove his love for her? If you're like me, those are the moments when your heart does that aching pull inside. We soon find ourselves wanting so much for our lives to look like what we see on the screen. If only our soul mate would come!

■

Have you felt it lately too? Sometimes it's the romantic movie; sometimes it's the young couple in front of you at church (while the seat next to you is empty); sometimes it's a song on the radio or a lonely evening at home. But it comes. And it feels so incredibly poignant and unlike anything you've ever experienced that it is strangely wonderful and bitterly awful at the same time. If ever there is a feeling that defies the bounds of this planet, it is the intensity of a heart aching to be fully known and to be pursued by a relentless love.

Complete

Phrases like "other half," "soul mate," and "better half" and lines from movies that sounded heaven sent (like "You complete me") all led me to believe the lie that I was incomplete. Suddenly, I was either too much or not enough—or worse, both at the same time. Not only did this new revelation make me feel like a total mess in my relationships with guys, but I was a total mess in general. I was walking around feeling un-whole because I was unable to find someone to fill the vacancy inside of me. I was heartbroken because the relationships I did have didn't last. It made me miserable and desperate. I would get stuck in "pits of despair" for months, wishing I could crawl out of the darkness and depression but not able to get a grip on the muddy walls to pull myself up.

I wish I could have stepped outside my body and seen myself. Like a person who looked in a mirror and then forgot what she looks like (James 1:23–25), I had forgotten the truth. I was so deceived—thinking I knew what was real about myself—but all along, it wasn't real at all. I thought I was half of what I need to be, but if had I looked into the mirror of God's Word, I would have seen my true reflection.

There was nothing incomplete about me. I was whole.

·

Does that surprise you? Have you been walking around with the mirage of a gaping hole in your heart, thinking you are incomplete? There is a beautiful truth I want you to know: the only holes in us are God-shaped ones. He is the only piece that can be missing to make you incomplete. He is the only piece that makes the unfinished puzzle total. And He is yours. If you believe in Christ and His sacrifice for you, then He has made you complete. WHOLE. Not lacking anything.

Now, you're probably wondering that if your heart still aches during romantic movies, how can this be? How can you be whole? Good question!

I struggled with this for a long, long time. Here's what I discovered: While God has made us entirely whole in Him, He still allows us to hunger and yearn for certain desires within our hearts. The pull on your heart to be a wife, to follow your dreams, to use your talents and achieve goals . . . these things are gifts, *but gifts do not add to or subtract from making you complete.* Just as we learned that checking off to-dos on our lists for life cannot fulfill us in some magical way, gaining the desires of our hearts cannot make us a more complete person than we are right now.

BUT—God has an incredible place and purpose for these desires of our hearts, and in the next chapter, we will see just how amazing these yearnings can be in their proper place. First, though, we must see the MOST astounding thing. So, for just a minute, consider this:

If there were someone relentlessly pursuing you with the truest and most passionate love,

- would it change how you see yourself and your life?
- would it be your dream come true?
- would it feel like the key that unlocks the indescribable ache in your heart?

YEAH! It would for me!

What if I told you that there is? that "for real," Someone is chasing after you because He can't stand to be without you? (Did your heart just make that little twinge and your stomach surge with butterflies?)

Well, the truth of the matter is that if there is one thing you can absolutely count on, it's that *you* are the object of Someone's deepest desire.

God says so:

> "Behold, I have engraved you on the palms of My hands."
> (Isaiah 49:16a)

THE COST

If someone were to ask you to measure true love, how would you do it? Perhaps by how passionately one feels for another? (But feelings can fade.) Perhaps by how consumed with daydreams they are of their loved one? (But daydreams can float away.) **Perhaps by the cost paid to *prove* their love?**

One of the greatest blessings I ever received was a broken heart.

Yep, you can reread that if you'd like! A broken heart and the broken hope of being a wife. But my broken heart was one of the best things that could have happened to me. I couldn't see it that way when I was in the midst of it; the weeks of tears didn't allow me to see much of anything. But it was through this event in my life that God opened my heart to the most captivating truth I've ever known.

You see, my boyfriend and I thought we'd marry each other. That is the thing we both wanted most—our end-aim. At first, it seemed to be a perfect fit, and we were delighted with the idea of having each other. But as time passed, we soon realized that we didn't see eye to eye on some very big issues. As we broke up, the words "just don't fit" popped out from both of us. It was the truth. I didn't fit with his friends, in his field of work, in his lifestyle. And while I was prepared to mold my life around him, it was obvious that I was too much of a square peg for the round hole of his life.

Let me tell you now that it was a very good thing that we didn't get married, for not every couple should try to make their lives fit together permanently. While it was not God's will for us to mold our futures to each other's, it was God's will to use our time together to show me something incredibly valuable and precious. What God revealed drastically changed my outlook on love. It hit me a few days after my boyfriend and I said our final good-byes.

August 24, 2011

Relationships were made to mirror Christ and His Bride (all believers). And that got me thinking—we didn't fit into Christ's lifestyle. We were separated, in every sense of the word, by our differences. So, He did everything He could to make it possible for us to fit—for us to belong. It was a long and arduous process—but He spent thirty-three years creating a way for His Bride to belong to Him. And an eternity orchestrating it before that.

He could have taken a thirty-three-year vacation on the Sea of Galilee, leaving and forgetting the Bride that didn't fit. But He loved her too much. He wanted her too much. And it cost Him everything. He left home to get her. Their forever-union in the end would be worth it.

And she knew how much she meant to Him; there was no doubt. No second-guessing His affections or devotion or faithfulness, because He proved there was no one and nothing that meant more than her.

And the consummation of that devotion is His glory; it is truly "glorious" for them both.

> Nothing less than everything—
> proved she meant the world to Him.

If we had fit perfectly into His life—no sacrifice, no molding, no adapting, no laying-down—then how little we would know He loved us.

By us being the square peg for His round-circle life, He could prove just how genuine, just how immense, just how exclusive His love was. And that is how He won her heart.

And that is what she wanted. She could have fit into many men's lives—but that made her convenient—not loved. "Greater love has no one than this, that someone lay down his life for his friends," Jesus said (John 15:13).

> The sacrifice measures the cost; the cost measures the depth of His love.

The Most Extravagant Romance

By losing a relationship, I gained a new perspective of the immensity of what I did have—the undying and relentless love of Christ. By being rejected, my heart was cut open enough for the wonder of my Heavenly Husband to overflow into it. I had to taste a tiny bit of the great cost of love.

One man wasn't willing to go the distance for me, but One already had. One had sought me as if He were seeking gold. I was His treasure. And He proved it by doing the unthinkable—He died for me. The story doesn't end in romantic tragedy of course. Instead, His death opened the way for me to be with Him forever. He wrote my "happily ever after."

> "For I am the LORD your God,
>   the Holy One of Israel, your Savior.
> I give Egypt as your ransom,
>   Cush and Seba in exchange for you.
> Because you are precious in My eyes,
>   and honored, and I love you."
>
> (Isaiah 43:3–4a)

And this is your story too. The ache in your heart has told you there is more—it yearns to be desired. It pulls and stretches inside of you. And it has been perfectly answered by the cross.

The story of your Lover is a reality. He has come. And He comes personally again in the water and Word of your "wedding day": your Baptism. The cost of His love for you not only proved its depth, it made you whole. Complete. Without blemish. As white as the most spotless wedding gown. Christ has brought you communion (relationship) with God Himself. All the barriers have been broken, and you are His.

He relentlessly pursued you and won you! What a love story! Hollywood has nothing even close to that level of romance! And get this: He *keeps* pursuing you as your beauty captivates Him anew every day! His passion for you will never fade.

When I understood that the cross held this for me, I was breathless. I understood that the cross canceled out my sin-debt, it put an *X* through the formulas of worldly beauty and success, and it gave new meaning to my "list of life." But to think that the cross held a story of divine romance *for me?*

Now, that did something real to my heart. It fulfilled my soul.

> "And I will betroth you to Me forever. I will betroth you to Me in righteousness and in justice, in steadfast love and in mercy. I will betroth you to Me in faithfulness. And you shall know the LORD." (Hosea 2:19–20)

THE GLORY OF GROWING

God has established a relationship with you. (That sentence alone is awe inspiring!) And one of the most exciting parts about this lifelong relationship is cultivating and growing it. God doesn't want to have a stagnant relationship with you; He wants you to fall more in love with Him every day. So how does one do that? Well, here are some fun suggestions for immersing yourself in your romance with Christ:

- Read Song of Solomon. Especially if you are new to thinking of Christ as your Husband, this is a great place to start! Read it from a study Bible for extra insight.

- Set aside time in the morning to read the Bible. Think of this *devotion* time as a quiet morning moment with your Heavenly Husband before the day begins.

- Think of church like a date! Instead of getting dressed up to look your best for others, think of it like you're getting ready to go spend time with your beloved King.

- Watch a sunset. Or set your alarm early to catch a sunrise. You'll be surprised at how time spent just pondering God's beauty will move your heart to adore Him even more.

- When you see the color green (the color of jealousy) throughout your day, make a point of remembering that God is jealous for you!

- Write love letters to God.

- Do something He has gifted you to do. One of my best friends loves to run, and she says it helped give her time to focus on God. And when I skate, my heart soars with the love of my Creator! Find what gives you a special moment with your Lord.

- Listen to Christian radio instead of songs that focus on relationships gone wrong and rejection. God-focused songs will be like prayers that delight your heart in God. (And there are ALL types and genres of Christian bands, from hip-hop to metal to rock to pop—and they are about as far from cheesy as you can imagine.)

- When you get up in the morning, make the sign of the cross over your chest to remember your Baptism—the day Christ united you to Himself. Take a second to be assured that nothing in this day can separate you from that extravagant love (Romans 8:37–39).

- Make your world and your every moment about your Heavenly Husband and your relationship with Him. Be joyous over knowing your "soul's Mate"! Live like your dream of finding true love has truly come true. Rest assured He will provide all other good things for your heart!

- Look into the mirror of God's Word daily to see the reflection of the prize He treasures. Let **it** do the creating of a strong relationship within you between you and your Lover.

Pocket It

Write out these verses for your pocket (or type them out on a notebook app and store in your phone):

Week 6:

- Jeremiah 31:3
- Isaiah 54:5
- Psalm 135:4
- Isaiah 62:5b
- Hosea 2:19–20

Week 7:

- Isaiah 61:10
- Psalm 23:6
- Isaiah 54:10
- Isaiah 62:12
- Psalm 63:3

CHAPTER FOUR

Beautiful Feet and a Hannah Heart

"How beautiful are the feet of those who preach the good news!"
(Romans 10:15b)

What do your feet look like? No, I'm not asking if you had a pedi recently. I'm simply wondering what's on your feet.

Mine have skates on. They are scuffed and worn—with gouges and holes from toepicks, and laces that used to be white.

What are on your feet? Maybe dressy flats? Or perhaps skateboard sneakers? How about ballet slippers or cowboy boots? (I'm from Montana; we wear those a lot around here.)

And where are those feet of yours going today? Walking to school? Entering the gym? Traversing dusty hiking trails? Perhaps they are tapping out rhythms or dancing under your chair.

No matter what adorns those appendages of yours, they are beautiful—for they are the carriers of some incredible news!

A Skater?!

When you're a little kid, you dream about what you'll be when you grow up. When I was very young, I had a list of occupations I planned to have. I actually wrote them all down at one point. It looked something like this:

- Teacher
- Book writer
- Missionary
- Barrel racer
- Body builder (If you could see my skinny arms now, you'd laugh!)
- Librarian
- Singer (Oh boy, I can't even carry a tune in a bucket; what was I thinking?!)
- AND . . . figure skater

With each passing year of my childhood, I knew more and more that the deepest desire on my heart was to be a skater. By the time I was in high school, I had worked out a plan to pursue my dream to seriously train as an ice dancer. But soon I was hearing a peculiar question: "A *figure skater?*"

You see, not only were the odds against me ever achieving such a goal, but it just wasn't what people thought would serve the Lord the best. A deaconess, a church worker, a teacher in a Christian school—all those seemed like obvious choices. But choosing to be an athlete and artist . . . well, that didn't look like the godliest thing to do.

But there was this incredible burning passion inside of me that I just couldn't explain. When I skated, I felt like my heart was . . . soaring! Every fiber of my being longed to be on the ice. It was home.

I knew I was meant to do this, but the skepticism of people around me raised doubts in my mind. Was I choosing to not serve the Lord? or serve Him less? Would God be happy with me if I were a skater? Would I miss God's plan if I wasn't a church worker? Was I wasting my faith on an athletic career?

All of these fears were agonizing for me. They circled in my head until my heart raced and my stomach churned. I wanted more than anything to believe that I could be an effective tool for God to use as a figure skater—that I could reach others through my talent. But I couldn't be certain it was true.

I remember the day the Lord told me.

I was sitting at my little green desk in my room, feeling like the weight of all the world was vacuuming the breath from my lungs. I said a prayer in sheer desperation. And I will never forget what happened next.

I opened my Bible, and there was 1 Corinthians 12. Every word was like golden assurance straight from God's lips. It was the first time I can clearly remember Him speaking directly to me through His Word. And it was incredible.

Now there are varieties of gifts, but the same Spirit; and there are varieties of service, but the same Lord; and there are varieties of activities, but it is the same God who empowers them all in everyone. (1 Corinthians 12:4–6)

I read on.

For just as the body is one and has many members, and all the members of the body, though many, are one body, so it is with Christ. . . .

For the body does not consist of one member but of many. If the foot should say, "Because I am not a hand, I do not belong to the body," that would not make it any less a part of the body. (1 Corinthians 12:12, 14–15)

That's ME! I'm like the foot! I thought . . . and I read on.

If the whole body were an eye, where would be the sense of hearing? If the whole body were an ear, where would be the sense of smell? But as it is, God arranged the members in the body, **each one of them, as He chose.** If all were a single member, where would the body be? As it is, there are many parts, yet one body. (1 Corinthians 12:17–20)

And it got even better!

The eye cannot say to the hand, "I have no need of you," nor again the head to the feet, "I have no need of you." On the contrary, the parts of the body that seem to be weaker **are indispensable,** and on those parts of the body that we think less honorable we bestow the greater honor. . . .

Now **you are** the body of Christ and individually members of it. (1 Corinthians 12:21–23a, 27; emphasis mine)

It seemed too good to be true. But it *was* true. It was *the* Truth.

As I write this, I am sitting at that same little green desk in that same room. Some of those very verses still hang on my wall, with a picture of a figure skater, her arms open wide to a globe and a cross. The years after I read those verses brought many things—hours upon hours of doing what I loved most, thousands of miles traveled, various training centers and coaches, two gold medals in my respective disciplines, ice shows and competitions, students and classes, triumphs and heartaches, tears and joy. But most of all, those years were held in the hand of a God who *delighted* in using the desire of my heart for His fame. And He showed me just how amazing His loving plan for me was—and is.

As I've told you, my life didn't play out exactly as I planned. My list of to-dos didn't get checked off as I thought they would, and my goal of being an Olympic champion was never realized.

But I wouldn't have it any other way.

∙

I wish you could step into my heart right now and know the presence of a God who works all things for our good and truly grants the longings of our hearts in Him. I can only hope this book gives you a mere glimpse of it. And I hope that you ask Him to reveal it personally to you.

It will captivate you!

I've never known such a beautiful peace and delight, and I wouldn't have been able to know it, had my "list of life" been followed according to my plan. But our mighty God wrote an amazing plotline for my little life as a figure skater—a life full of His protection and guidance and comfort and intimacy and provision. And as I look back, just over twenty-four short years of living, I see a God who took the gift He gave me and brought about the true desires of my heart by writing a story that was about Him and His love for me in Christ. I am not an Olympic gold medalist; there are no world championship titles after my name. But every day I get to worship my Lord on the ice and pass on to my beloved students the love of a conquering Christ and the experience He has given me in this sport. And He hasn't stopped there. My faith in Him allows me to look forward to a future that continues to take my breath away. He is opening doors to avenues of ministry through skating and choreography, and even to this day, when I step onto a sheet of ice, I know the hand of my God.

What's on **Your** Beautiful Feet?

Do you remember my questions at the beginning of this chapter—what do your feet look like and where are they taking you? Can you think of people you come in contact with through your everyday activities who need to hear the Good News you can share?

Here's my next question: What makes *your* heart soar? What has God planted inside of you that causes your face to beam with a smile and your pulse to quicken?

Think about the things you love to do most. Have you ever considered that they are *tools?* that they are divine instruments with a heavenly purpose? that they are more than simple hobbies or interests on which to spend your time?

What if your gifts could make a difference for the kingdom of God? That sounds like a royal purpose, doesn't it?! The truth is, **you are part of the Body of Christ, and He has** gifted you in a special way. The Word of God cannot lie, and it says that you have been given an important function in the Body and that God Himself chose it specifically for you. Reread that sentence. Do you feel the immensity of it? The verses from 1 Corinthians 12 were written thousands of years before you were born. And yet, God knew He would plant a gift inside of you, "as He chose" (v. 18).

∙

There have been moments in my life when I found myself reverting to culture's formulas for life—times when I again listened to the messages of the world more than the voice of God. One of those moments came after I had trained as an ice dancer and then spent some time in an ice show. I listened to the cultural message that I had accomplished what I set out to do as a child, but that now it was time to grow up and plug myself into the normal lifestyles of the typical American. I figured that I had had an extraordinary life as an athlete, and now I should be like everyone else and should follow the standard to-do list.

Funny thing was, I didn't fit. I spent several years trying to find a spot where I could belong—I enrolled in college, changed my major several times, and eventually never went. I got a full-time job doing something I hardly enjoyed. I sought out every idea possible—some of them great, like Bible college. But I always came back to the fact that I didn't believe God was leading me there.

It was a priceless time in my life, actually, because I learned what it meant to fully surrender my plans to God. I needed direction, and I knew it wasn't going to come from within me or from the pressures of society. It had to come from Him. And in due time, He revealed it. Guess what? He gave me a place where I had belonged all along, serving Him with my life on the ice.

∙

What about you? Is the world telling you what you should be? What kind of step-by-step plan does the world say you should follow? Has it become louder in your ears than what God is whispering to your heart? Do your feet look like unusual suspects for work in the kingdom of God?

Not everything we plan to pursue becomes what we do with our lives. Just look at the list of careers I had as a child; I like horses and music and books, but I wasn't meant to be a barrel racer, singer, or librarian.

So, how *do* you know? How do you figure out what you're supposed to do with your gifts and which ones to use when?

Ask. Sit back down at the foot of that cross and ask your Savior to hold your gifts in His hand. Ask Him to show you what you are supposed to do each step of the way. Ask Him to keep showing you through every season of your life.

Christ will not grant perfect clarity. I've learned that. He's not in the business of revealing a ten-year plan to you . . . much less a thirty-year plan! But He will show you day by day what His purpose is for you. If you stay connected to Him through His Word and seek His face daily through prayer, He will illuminate the path before you and lead you right where He wants you. And I can tell you, when you look back someday and see how He brought you to where you are— even if the road was bumpy—you'll stand in awe.

> I cry out to God Most High,
> > to God who fulfills His purpose for me.
>
> (Psalm 57:2)

I want to propose something to you. Instead of joining the anthem of the world to "follow your heart," let's sit at our Jesus' feet and ask that He enable us to "follow *His* heart." I guarantee you'll find that **what He brings about is the truest desire of your heart.** For God the Son knows you better than even you do. And He knows the genuine longings in your heart even more than you do. He's the one who put them there.

AT HIS FEET

O Beloved Savior,

I am here at Your feet to hear You. Your Word says that You have given to me a purpose and a gift, a place to belong and serve in Your Body. I want to be an instrument for Your mercy and Your grace. Show me Your will for my life. Make it Your life—not mine. Reveal to me how You want me to use the gifts You've given me, and please lead me day by day in Your path. Take my talents, gifts, interests, passions, and desires of my heart and forever hold them in Your almighty hands. Write my story, Lord. And when I stumble along the way, forgive me and please pick me back up. Renew my passion for taking Your Good News into all the world, and give me the strength I need. Most of all, delight my heart in You, and thereby show me the truest desires of my heart.

I love You, Lord.

Amen.

YOUR WORLD A MISSION FIELD

During the time I was praying to know God's will for my life as a young skater, I wrote a poem that would become my mission statement. It hung on my wall in the various cities, dorms, and rooms I lived in while training and is still a reminder to me today:

Lord, I heard Thy call
When it came to me
Not with bugles triumphantly
But with the calmest whisper
Stirred inside my heart
Lord, Thy call to do my part

An ambassador for Christ
Is what I'm to be
A rink as my embassy
To shine as I show this world
God's precious gift to me
Lord, the glory all to Thee

To skate, to be the best
My heart happiest inside of me
Lord, Thy blessing makes me free!
To fly on wings like eagles
Christ's power inside of me
I skate for Thee

Take some time this week to think about what you would write as your own mission statement or poem. It may be as simple as "Lord, show me what You want for me." Write it down and post it on your wall or in your locker at school.

Hannah Heart

I would like you to meet Hannah.

Hannah was a girl who's heart held an aching desire and who saw that desire fulfilled.

Read her story in 1 Samuel 1, and then let's talk about her.

■

Have you read it? Good. Hannah was an interesting woman, wasn't she? Does anything in her story seem striking to you? A lot, right?! When I came across her story again a few years back, it hit me as if I'd never read it before. The Scripture account of Samuel's mother seemed to open a locked door to the mysteries of my own heart, and I found myself searching it intently to see if I could discover what God was saying to me through her life.

He said a lot. And I'm pretty sure He told me so I could tell you.

Hannah had an ache. There was something she wanted more than anything else in the world. What was it? A son . . . well, kinda. You see, Hannah was one of the wives of Elkanah, and she was barren, which means she was unable to have children, and having children just happened to be the thing she wanted most. In those days, a wife was supposed to have children and if a wife didn't, then people thought God was punishing her for some deep, dark sin. To make matters worse, Hannah's rival, Peninnah, the other wife of Elkanah, was constantly provoking her and rubbing it in her face that she couldn't have a child.

The ache in Hannah's heart must have seemed unbearable. It must have resounded so deeply within her chest that her very soul was distressed. She poured out the pain in a stream of tears. And not just any tears. You know the kind—the ones that come from some unearthly place inside of you. Some place where only you fully know the vastness of your longing—wide and long and hollow-feeling. Those kinds of aches seem as if they are a black hole, opening broadly into untouched depths and swallowing everything in you.

I've had mine. Have you had yours? These aches come with questions; questions like, Why has God let me long for this if it isn't meant to be? Why doesn't He hear the echo of this desire inside my heart? Why do I have to feel this? Why doesn't He *do* something?

And Hannah had hers: Why has my God caused me to be barren and yet let me desire so much to have a son?

Why? Because of something incredibly beautiful. Keep reading; we'll get there!

•

Have you ever felt guilty about your longings? Maybe you long to be married, or to follow a dream, or to accomplish something. We've already talked about how you have everything you need to be complete in Christ and that your to-do lists won't fulfill you. So why in the world would we ever long for anything else? We are already full. God fills every void. We are whole . . . and yet, we ache.

Hannah ached too. And the question from her husband must have seemed like a dagger of guilt:

> "Hannah, why do you weep? And why do you not eat? And why is your heart sad? *Am I not more to you than ten sons?*" (1 Samuel 1:8; emphasis mine)

Have you ever heard a similar question inside your own brain? You feel ashamed to want something; "God should be enough," you reason. "Isn't God worth *'more . . . than ten sons'?* worth more than my desire!?"

I sometimes imagine that Hannah responded to Elkanah like this:

"Yes! Yes, you *do* mean more to me than ten sons! More than a thousand sons!! And that's just it, Elkanah. That's one reason this hurts so much. I can't explain it. I think my heart is in the right place—and yet I still long so much for this! Can't anyone see that I don't love you less? that this doesn't negate my love for you? that this isn't wrong?"

Eli, the priest, did see. You wanna know how we can know that? As Hannah was in the temple praying, Eli saw her. At first he thought she was an intoxicated and delirious visitor who had had far too much wine. But when he approached her, he found quite the opposite. Hannah explained that she had not been drinking at all, but rather she was "pouring out [her] soul before the Lord" (v. 15). And that's when Eli saw it—her heart.

"Do not take your servant as a wicked woman," Hannah begged.

I've sat at the feet of my Savior, and on the couch of my pastor's study, begging the same thing. "Don't take me as an evil girl for longing for this; I do love my God! My ache doesn't lessen that! Right?"

I love Eli's response to Hannah: "Go in peace, and the God of Israel grant your petition that you have made to Him" (v. 17).

What I love most is not that Eli says he hopes God answers her prayer; it's that he doesn't condemn her for longing for something. He could see that her heart was truly in the right place—with God first. He never would have sent her away with a blessing if he thought her desire had replaced God and become her idol.

Hannah responds, "Let your servant find favor in your eyes" (v. 18). Her humble servant-heart still wished to be *right* in his sight, right in the sight of this man of God, right in the sight of God Himself and without fault or sin. And when Eli sent her away, I think he sent her away with much more than a priestly benediction and blessing. I believe he sent her away with a firm reassurance for her own heart that she was not wronging her God.

∎

Haven't you wished for the same thing? Don't you want to know that your aches and longings and desires don't make you a traitor in God's sight? I know I have. When I was a teenager, I had desires on my heart that I thought beyond a doubt were true and noble and of God. They weren't. And God revealed that in time. But as I grew in my relationship with Him, He truly began to make Himself first in my life. So when I was confronted with the gnawing of deep longings again, I was skeptical and scared at first. I knew my heart could lie (as it had in the past—big time!) and that I really needed to keep myself strongly connected to Him. It was then that God showed me *Hannah heart*.

∎

Let's take a look at Hannah's heart for a minute. We know a few things about it: It intensely longed to have a son. It desired more than anything to be a mother. It was humble and had God in first place.

But there are a few things we question: Why did her heart ache so much for this specific thing? And why, if she wanted a son so badly, did she vow to give him up to the Lord if she ever bore him? (See v. 11.) It doesn't seem to make any sense! Why would she want a son if she was just going to give him up forever anyway?

There are a few possibilities. She could have just wanted to get Peninnah to close her hurtful mouth at last, or maybe she simply wanted to experience being a mother, even if for just a short time. But I don't think that either of those was the reason for the ache in her soul. Peninnah would have found something else to hound Hannah about, and tasting motherhood for a few months wouldn't have satisfied Hannah.

I believe Hannah ached to have a son because the ache was directly **tied** to her God.

I bet you've heard Christians say that our desires point us to God (didn't I just say that too?). And it's true. Our longings move us toward the One who can fill every void. We've learned that. Desires can be great guideposts and signs that point smack-dab to our Creator, Sustainer, and Lover. Desiring a husband or boyfriend can point us to our Heavenly Husband, and desiring to achieve a goal can point us to what God has already done for us. During my teenage years (those times I was talking about when my heart lied big time), I learned this firsthand. I found that my longing for a certain guy was God's way of opening a doorway into the truth of all God could be to me. He used my desire to show me how much I was created to desire God Himself. That teenage longing of mine went unrealized. (Thank God it did!) It was a tool that the Lord used. But there are other times when our longings are not only tools that *point* to Him, but are *tied* to Him.

Go ahead and read 1 Samuel 2 now—Hannah's Prayer.

Look at the first line of her song: "My heart exults in the Lord" (v. 1). She has been given the desire of her heart, a son, and instead of starting off by singing "My heart rejoices in having my desire fulfilled," her first thought is of her God. As we read her entire song of praise, we can see it is actually a song *about her relationship with God.*

•

Hannah's longing was directly tied to that relationship with her God. Remember when I asked you at the beginning of this section (page 65) what Hannah desired most of all? Well, her desire wasn't only about a son—it was *about God.*

True, God could fill every nook and cranny of her soul regardless of whether she was a mother or not, but God had a specific plan for this ache of hers. He used it to *reveal more of Himself* intimately to Hannah (and to us)—His love, His power, His ways of working against the odds, His ability to touch the depths of her being, His delight in lifting up the lowly. But He didn't stop there; Hannah's longed-for son, Samuel, became a prophet of Israel and anointed Saul as king. Saul was replaced by David. David's descendant was Joseph, the husband of Mary—a virgin girl from Nazareth who became the mother of Jesus Christ, the longed-for Messiah. One little longing, within one little heart, in one little-known girl in the hill country of Ephraim was what God used to set in motion His plan of salvation.

Wow.

The desire burning inside of Hannah was given to her by God. We can see that, standing where we are today. But Hannah knew only that her very soul was crying out to be a mother. And the Lord used that ache not just for her to experience something temporary but for all believers to experience something eternal.

•

How do you know that your heart is like a Hannah heart and in the right place? Consider if you would do what she did—would you give up your deepest desire to the Lord for "all the days" (1 Samuel 1:11)? Would you let your desire be dedicated to Him? Would you be willing to lay it at His feet, although it aches like the thing you want most?

Hannah vowed to give up her child to the Lord forever because that desire was tied to THE deepest desire of her heart—loving her God above all else. It can seem backward to us, especially when our hearts are burning and crying out with such passion! We often don't feel like surrendering our greatest wants. But if our desires are from God, they will certainly be safe in the hands that formed them! And if they are not from God, then putting them under the soil at the foot of Christ's cross is the perfect place to bury them. And I guarantee, just as it was for Hannah, that when God is the **deepest** desire inside your soul, your heart will truly rejoice in all that He brings!

■

You know what makes me smile most when I read this story of Hannah? Not only was she not wrong in desiring something; and not only did God hear her prayer and do the impossible by opening her closed womb; and not only did He make her son, Samuel, a key player in bringing about His plan of salvation—but He did one more thing. Open your Bible right now and read 1 Samuel 2:20–21.

Didn't that make you smile?! "The Lord was gracious to Hannah" (NIV). Other translations say, "The Lord *visited* Hannah." This amazing God, who heard the cry of some seemingly unimportant girl, came to her. He could have forgotten about her after she bore the prophet Samuel. He had what He needed to set in motion His mission to bring Christ to earth. But He didn't forget; He *remembered* her. The aches of her heart weren't unimportant to Him; He touched them, and He gave her two daughters and three more sons.

The beautiful story of Hannah not only shows us her heart, but most important, it shows us God's:

Therefore the Lord longs to be gracious to you,
And therefore He waits on high to have compassion on you.
For the LORD is a God of justice;
How blessed are all those who **long for Him.**

(Isaiah 30:18 [NASB]; emphasis mine)

Making It Real in Your Life

I can't believe I'm going to tell you this, but here it goes!

I once felt very strongly about a certain guy in my life. (You're probably wondering by now how many of these guys there were in my young adult life! A handful or so.) I was so sure about the way I felt toward this person that I began to believe I couldn't live without this relationship. That's when God asked me to lay my desire down. He enabled me to—literally. There's an old wooden cross outside my bedroom window that my family had put up one Christmas a couple years back to hang lights on. And early one morning, before anyone was awake, I buried a tin can in the soil under that cross. In the can was a letter to God. I told Him about how strongly I felt about the situation, how I thought I knew what my heart wanted, and how I now was surrendering this desire to Him. I told Him that He could do whatever He wanted with it . . . and I buried it.

A week or two later, I looked out across the yard to the foot of the cross. A HOLE! What!? Our dogs had apparently been sniffing around my prayer-in-a-tin-can and had tried to unearth it. They weren't entirely successful, fortunately! I hurried to get a shovel and packed some dirt back down on top of the spot.

The mischief of the dogs proved to be an important lesson to me. Ironically, at that same time, I was really struggling with keeping that desire surrendered to God and not taking matters into my own hands. It was one of those times when I knew God was telling me to let Him write my story and that I needed to stop grasping for the pen in His hands. He had not given me any green lights on the situation, and the half-dug hole reminded me that I had no business taking up my desire unless He was the one who placed it back in my hands.

∎

What about you? Is there something pressing in on your heart so strongly that it feels unbearable? Is there a dream or goal or person that makes your heart ache? Have you visited the foot of the cross lately? The good news is you don't have to possess the willpower to surrender your desires to Him. **His Spirit inside of you will enable you** to do that as you seek Him in His Word and take His body and blood in Holy Communion and as you pray. Ask Him to fill you and to move your heart in the path of His will.

> I will instruct you and teach you in the way you should go;
> I will counsel you with My eye upon you.
>
> (Psalm 32:8)

∎

One more story? And this one doesn't involve tin cans or dogs.

When I left competitive skating and professional ice shows in my early twenties, I couldn't dispel the passion for skating that was still in my heart. I didn't know how God could possibly use it in the new place I was in my life. So there was a season of waiting. (Much of my skating career has been a season of waiting!) I wasn't sure what God was going to do with the desire in my heart to continue performing, but I waited, and He helped me keep my longing at His feet. Wanna know what happened next? He *remembered* me. He *visited* me. He longed to be gracious to me, and He rose to show me compassion. He took my little heart's cry and turned it into the song of Hannah! He opened doors that seemed to appear out of nowhere, and He unlocked ways for me and my skating that I had never seen before.

He gave me the desire of my heart in a way I wouldn't have expected, and "My heart rejoices in my God!" is now *my* song!

∎

Has there been a time in your life when the Lord touched the desires in your heart in a breathtaking way? Ask some of your family members or adult friends at church if they have stories of God hearing their heart's cry. I bet you'll find that the way God answers each is uniquely marvelous!

POCKET IT

Delight in His promises. Spend some time looking up each of these Scripture passages; there is no better way to sit at His feet!

Week 8:

- Psalm 4
- Ephesians 3:20–21
- Psalm 16
- Psalm 31:14–24
- Psalm 18:16–19
- Psalm 69:32

WRITE A PRAYER OF SURRENDER

No tin can or wooden cross needed—just take out a pen and tell your Lord exactly how you feel, what is on your heart, and how you want Him to be the one to whom all your desires are tied!

Father God,

CHAPTER FIVE

Garden

I have a small bouquet of flowers on my windowsill. They were given to me this morning as an Easter present. So simple. Petals and stems. But they are striking to me as they sit there in the sun. *Why?* I found myself wondering. My answer was rather simple too— because they are *beautiful*.

You, too, my dear friend, are striking because of your beauty. Just like the flowers on my windowsill, you are the image of something precious and captivating. Something that speaks the very way those daisies do. Something that is infinitely beautiful. But you are not just a bouquet of flowers or even one long-stem rose—you are a **garden**.

Can you see it? Think of Jane Austen times in eighteenth-century England and imagine the grand and romantic "secret" gardens with rustic wooden doors under mossy archways and walls of stone upon stone so stately that only the garden keeper knows fully what is kept inside. From the outside, you can't help but notice the way the winding vines seem to weave and dance to the very top and how hints of pastel-colored blooms peek into the sky. Sweet blossom fragrances sweep into the wind as you walk by, making your heart thoroughly delighted in such a wondrous and mysterious place.

You are that place.

You are the beautiful and walled garden. Have you ever thought of yourself that way? As we've mentioned earlier, not many of us feel very beautiful or captivating at all. We use other words to describe ourselves, don't we? Words like *frumpy, fat, ugly, awkward, disproportioned, unattractive.* But take a closer look at that garden wall . . . do you see the little wooden plaque hanging near the door?

Song of Solomon 4:12:
A garden locked is my sister, my bride,
a spring locked, a fountain sealed.

Take a second and open your Bible to Song of Solomon (or Song of Songs) 4. Let's keep reading verses 13–14:

Your shoots are an orchard of pomegranates
with all choicest fruits,
henna with nard,
nard and saffron, calamus and cinnamon,
with all trees of frankincense,
myrrh and aloes,
with all choice spices.

Wow. Sounds like a pretty amazing planting! Even if you aren't familiar with all those plants and fragrances listed in the passage, you can imagine how vibrant and lush and full of life that garden is! It sounds like a place of divine delight.

■

In the Bible, God calls you a garden . . . a "watered" garden (Isaiah 58:11; Jeremiah 31:12).

He calls you "the planting of the Lord, that He may be glorified" (Isaiah 61:3b).

■

Knowing that this is what you ARE can make a huge difference in how you see yourself, your past and future, and your relationships. Let's take a look together at why this truth is so transforming.

INSIDE THE WALLS

All gardens can be pretty, but there is something especially alluring about a secret garden. In order to know all the wonder it holds, one has to somehow gain passage through the barricade of walls. And once inside, it's as if everything is more stunning and beautiful, simply because it is kept from the average eye. It is a world of its own.

Picture the borders of dense foliage. The deep green of the leaves, the intense red of the roses, the delicate white and sunny yellow of the daisies. Around each corner there is a new thing of beauty and mystery to behold. And with each new discovery, you remember that it is indeed "new"—no eyes have seen it, no feet have disturbed it, no hands have reached out for it. You begin to sense it is a place of honor—because it is a place no one else has been.

God intended your garden to be that way. Set apart.

Set apart for a specific purpose.

Set apart for a holy intention.

Set apart for a divinely beautiful function.

Your garden is the place where you and your husband consummate your marriage. In other words, the garden we speak of is SEX.

When I was your age, if I heard or even saw those three little letters—S E X—I would turn my head while my face transformed into a really amazing shade of pink and I would awkwardly fidget in my seat. But *sex* isn't some profane word or taboo subject. Don't make the mistake of thinking that sex is a topic off-limits to Christians. In fact, sex is one of God's favorite subjects! Did you know there is a whole book in the Bible about sex? Yep, Song of Solomon (the place where we've been reading these garden verses) is an entire book dedicated to the poetry of intimacy between a man and his bride.

Sex is God's good design. It was His idea! And God has made every person (even you and me) a sexual being. But, like every wonderful thing, our sexuality has to be taken care of, tended, and used properly. Instead of feeling like it is some shameful thing to be passed over, I pray you will find excitement in tending to it and cultivating it to be the place God intended it to be—a place of incredible beauty. And if you feel like perhaps you've already messed up your garden and it isn't so "set apart," keep reading!

UNTIL IT'S LIKE THIS

> I adjure you, O daughters of Jerusalem,
>   by the gazelles or the does of the field,
> that you not stir up or awaken love
>   until it pleases.
> (Song of Solomon 2:7)

"Until it pleases." In other words, "until it's like **this!"**

The woman in Song of Solomon knew what she was talking about. She was ever so in love. Smitten. Head-over-sandals. Completely mesmerized by her lover. But that's not what she meant when she told us to wait until love is "like this." No, there was much more behind her command.

Exclusiveness. She and her husband were **fully** dedicated to each other.

> My beloved is mine, and I am his. (Song of Solomon 2:16a)

There was no room in their relationship for intrusion from anyone else. They had become one. No longer two individuals who were merely interested in each other. They were united into **one** who were molded into one another—and her garden became his.

> My beloved has gone down to **his** garden
>   to the beds of spices,
> to graze in the gardens

and to gather lilies.
I am my beloved's and my beloved is mine;
   he grazes among the lilies.
(Song of Solomon 6:2–3; emphasis mine)

The Shulammite woman knew what it was to be in love. Just read her words in the song—she couldn't sleep, she daydreamed about how amazingly handsome and strong her lover was, her dreams were full of him when she did finally sleep, and her heart yearned to be with him every hour. She knew every aspect of the feeling of being in love.

But she also knew a much deeper side of love, deeper than feelings. She experienced complete commitment and union. And that is what she meant when she said, "Hey girls, wait until love is like this before you wake it!"

And I think that's what delights my heart the most about Song of Solomon. It isn't like God is telling us through their story that marriage must be a stern and rigid and unhappy thing. It isn't like He's saying, "This is serious business, and therefore, NO FUN, NO JOY, NO DAYDREAMING about how wonderful love is!" No, it's quite the opposite, isn't it? Just look at this couple in Song of Solomon. They were absolutely intoxicated with each other. Some of the most beautiful and exciting moments of their lives occurred in intimacy with their mate. They were thoroughly delighted in each other's garden and even more delighted to have given their gardens to each other forever. And God Himself was ever so delighted in their love! I believe Song of Solomon makes our Lord smile the widest grin. It's a picture of how He intended love and sex and marriage to be. He didn't plant a boring and lifeless garden with withered bushes and flowers in shades of brown; instead, He created a most captivating and sacred wonder for us to share in.

But that wonder isn't half what it should be when the complete commitment and union are missing. As we can see, sex is a celebration of being bonded inseparably together. It is a consummation of a covenant—**the act of sealing the sacred promise.** It includes the wonderful feelings of "being in love," but it is also much deeper than feelings.

While the emotions and feelings of being in love can sometimes lessen over time, the commitment that two people promise before God in their wedding vows is solid and unchanging. It is like the foundation that makes a house withstand every changing wind and storm. Love built upon the sand of emotions can be wonderful at first, but when the rains come, down it goes. Love built upon the Rock of Christ and the cement of exclusive commitment in Him might shake a bit when tornadoes come, but it won't go down. Sex is the physical, emotional, and spiritual act of strengthening that foundation, of deepening that bond.

Sounds beautiful, doesn't it?

Gardens full of remarkable discovery; hearts captivated by alluring love; vows of enduring union . . . but do you feel a twinge of sadness as you think about all this as well? I do. The delightfulness of love and marriage doesn't look all that beautiful in our lives sometimes, does it? Oh, we long for it to be this wonderful Song of Solomon place, but we are reminded daily of how sin has stained so much of what was supposed to be beautiful. We live in a fallen world. Sin not only affects our own hearts and homes; it affects God's good design for sex and marriage.

Sex has become something so twisted and out of place. It is no longer seen by our culture as a sealing of a holy promise; it's become merely a casual act, not a covenant. "Hookups" have made it a pastime, and boyfriends and girlfriends now often use sex as a test to see if they'd be compatible as a couple. Pornography has made secret gardens a thing of the past and has torn up roots where roses should have bloomed. Purity rings remain "in" for Christians, but are often on the hands of those seeking self-stimulation or oral sex. Sin and society have so distorted and bruised sex that we hardly see it clearly anymore. The lies of the world can start to seem like truth. And we often find ourselves right in the midst of them.

■

Let's take a look at some of the lies coming our way.

The World Says:

🚫 "It's okay as long as you love each other."

Sounds like a good boundary, but does it portray a Song of Solomon kind of love? And is it truly love if either person will go "all the way" in sex, but not "all the way" in vowed commitment?

🚫 "Promiscuity makes perfect."

The only thing promiscuity (casual sex with a number of partners) makes perfect is putting your bonding process in jeopardy for you and your future spouse. Scientific research has shown that the brain is greatly affected by sex *(Hooked: New Science on How Casual Sex is Affecting Our Children* by Joe S. McIlhaney Jr., M.D., and Freda McKissic Bush, M.D., Moody Publishers 2008). Yep, you read that right . . . the *brain!* When a person participates in physical intimacy with someone else, chemicals are released within the brain. Part of the job of these neurochemicals is to create a bond between sexual partners. The process of having sex, chemically bonding within the brain, breaking up, and having sex with someone else actually *molds* the brain in a very negative way. And over time, the brain comes to see this process of bonding and breaking as normal. That's not good news—especially when that person finds herself or himself wanting to be in a long-term relationship and feels she or he cannot commit to the other person. But the good news is that the brain is always moldable, even until death. With the Holy Spirit doing His redecorating inside our human hearts, He can lead us in remolding our brains through new healthy patterns of behavior and Christlike character.

🚫 "You'll be learning to love your future spouse by
   getting as much sexual experience as you can now."

Would it make you happy to know that in preparation for his
wedding night, your fiancé had slept with five other women? Happy
would be the last feeling I'd have! I'd be furious, disappointed, self-
conscious *(What if he thinks my garden doesn't match up to theirs?)*,
jealous . . . and betrayed. There's nothing about loving your future
spouse in "getting good" at sex. Now let me tell you a little secret:
you'll both figure it out when the time comes on your wedding night.
That will be half the joy of making your gardens one. Sex at its core
is about being completely exclusive—there's no prior experience
needed.

🚫 "Revealing some of the garden's goods don't hurt
   nothin'."

As a girl in today's society, it can feel like the more skin you
show, the more popular you are. In fact, when you're shopping, it can
be hard to find clothing that isn't revealing in some way. But let me
tell you, girl, that **MODesty** is in!!

The Book of Proverbs addresses a man by saying that his wife
shouldn't be on public display in a sexual way:

> Drink water from your own cistern,
>   flowing water from your own well.
> Should your springs be scattered abroad,
>   streams of water in the streets?
> Let them be for yourself alone,
>   and not for strangers with you.
> Let your fountain be blessed,
>   and rejoice in the wife of your youth.
>
> (Proverbs 5:15–18)

When we wear clothes that are revealing and suggest we're avail-
able for sexual interest, we are not doing our part in protecting the

eyes, hearts, and minds of guys around us. Just like we talked about earlier, our character is revealed in our actions. We cannot act (or dress) one way and *be* another. Choosing to get attention by showing off a little of our garden's goods may make us feel beautiful or desirable at first, but eventually we'll feel like we've exposed pieces of the sacred place meant only for our husband. Wouldn't we rather wait and give all of ourselves to that one man? And in the process, protect other girls' future husbands from thinking impure thoughts about us? Now, I'm not saying go stock up on turtlenecks and ankle-length skirts! I am saying, dress in a way that shows you care for the body your Lord has given you, that you consider it an honor to look good *and girly* while keeping your garden goods for only your husband's eyes. It can be a kinda fun challenge to be creative and put together current styles that are totally "in" and MODest at the same time. Do you have a blouse that's too low when you bend over? Then get a cute scarf to tie around your neck. Do you have pants that are practically painted to your backside? Then choose a little skirt to pull over them (you'll be totally "artsy"!). Do you have some shirts that are a bit too short? Then layer a cami underneath or a jacket over top. Try it! I bet you can pull off some incredible style and keep your garden's delights for your hubby! He'll appreciate it.

⊘ "Purity is only about not having sex until you're married."

Wrong. Purity lasts way beyond your wedding. The need for it doesn't go away when you replace a purity ring with a wedding band. In fact, purity is what *preserves a marriage.*

> Let marriage be held in honor among all, and let the marriage bed be undefiled. (Hebrews 13:4a)

Purity is about all of your life—not just sex. The actions you do during your everyday life will be brought to bed when you have sex with your husband. Since we cannot separate our sexuality from who we are as people, we cannot separate who we are and what we do from our sexuality. Sin can creep in and contaminate our thinking—say, through graphic romance novels, immoral movies that make God's design for sex seem outdated, or magazines that make forbidden affairs seem steamy and enticing. When this sin starts to plant seeds of wrong thinking in our minds, it can lead to some very devastating consequences. And when it's just you and your hubby all wrapped up in the sheets, you won't want those images or that type of thinking to be all wrapped up in there with you.

🚫 "You still keep your virginity if you just have oral sex."

Besides the growing number of cases of disease due to oral sex and other alternative activities, there are many other reasons why these loopholes won't preserve your purity. Even if a girl remains a "technical virgin" by abstaining from penetration, she can lose much of herself—and take much of her boyfriend's self—by participating in alternative sex. It isn't a matter of just "not crossing the line"; it's a matter of how we treat all aspects of sexual activity.

Think back to Song of Solomon. Do you think oral sex would fit in that poetry? Do you think it's something that could be celebrated for its intimacy and union and delight? No. It's merely a way of getting sexual urges met for the benefit of one's self. There's nothing about dedicating all of your body or heart to each other in this act.

Such loopholes are cracks in the garden wall. Instead of vowing a holy promise and coming through the gate, garden visitors are admitted for just a while through a loose brick. And the impression they leave is just as harmful as premarital sex.

🚫 "Everyone masturbates."

Self-stimulation isn't for everyone—it isn't for <u>anyone</u>! While the media and popular music make it seem like a normal solution for every person wanting to be sexually satisfied, masturbation is not part of God's design for sex. In fact, it can be incredibly damaging to the person engaging in it and to their mate. Just like the other loopholes we discussed, masturbation is all about *self*. Put it in the context of Song of Solomon . . . does it fit? Not at all. Sexual urges are normal and can seem overwhelming, but we must not turn something good into something self-serving and distorted.

> For this is the will of God, your sanctification: that you abstain from sexual immorality; that each one of you know how to control his own body in holiness and honor, not in the passion of lust like the Gentiles who do not know God; that no one transgress and wrong his brother in this matter, because the Lord is an avenger in all these things, as we told you beforehand and solemnly warned you. For God has not called us for impurity, but in holiness. Therefore whoever disregards this, disregards not man but God, who gives His Holy Spirit to you. (1 Thessalonians 4:3–8)

🚫 "Married sex is boring and second-rate."

I'm gonna give you a mission. During this week, count all the times you hear someone comment on TV about how boring and mundane married life is. You'll hear it and see it everywhere—commercials, sitcoms, cartoons, movies, characters wearing T-shirts with "ball and chain" written on them. The message from the world is clear on this one: married life is a chore, and married sex isn't half as much fun as sex outside of marriage. Wow, how far we've come from God's version! God designed married sex to be exhilarating and purposeful. Just listen to the guy in Song of Solomon:

> How beautiful and pleasant you are,
>   O loved one, with all your delights!
> (Song of Solomon 7:6)

He sounds rather excited, don't ya think?

Or what about this from the woman:

Set me as a seal upon your heart,
    as a seal upon your arm,
for love is strong as death,
    jealousy is fierce as the grave.
Its flashes are flashes of fire,
    the very flame of the Lord.
Many waters cannot quench love,
    neither can floods drown it.
If a man offered for love
    all the wealth of his house,
    he would be utterly despised.

(Song of Solomon 8:6–7)

The "blazing fire" of their love wasn't boring! Quite the opposite—it filled up a whole book in the Bible! *That's how God intended it to be.* Sure, things in this sinful world will drag us down, married life included. But that doesn't mean that the planting of joy and excitement and intimacy God has sown in marriage must wither more the longer two people live together. When God is the "third person" in your marriage, that blazing fire of love can burn brighter, not dimmer, and can grow *more beautiful* as time goes on!

"Catch for Us the Little Foxes": A Message from the Lover

"Catch the foxes for us,
    the little foxes
that spoil the vineyards,
    for our vineyards are in blossom."

(Song of Solomon 2:15)

That is the message from the lover to his beloved. That is the message from the husband to his wife. That is the message from your God to you. And that is the message from your future husband to you—today.

"Catch the little foxes." Who are they? *What* are they? The little foxes are all that could ruin the garden, everything that threatens to destroy the couple's bonded intimacy. And almost as a prayer, the lover admonishes his beloved to capture them before they are able to do any harm.

I love this verse, partly because it is the man asking the woman to play her part in preserving the garden. He is so intent on keeping their love pure and exclusive. Just verses before, he couldn't stop describing how much he longs for the sweetness of the sound of his wife's voice and the loveliness of her face. He truly loves her. And I also love this verse because it gives the woman something to actively **do** to enhance and protect their bond. This verse gives *me* something to do. As if from the lips of my future husband himself, I find great excitement in his wish that I prepare the garden and my heart by "catching the little foxes . . . *for us.*"

Watching for those little varmints is a daily thing. When seductive scenes in a movie pop onto the TV screen, I change the channel; when a song on the radio leads my mind in places it shouldn't be, I put in a CD; when I'm tempted to flirt with a guy just for the fun of it, I pray for my God to help me walk away.

Don't get me wrong; I'm no angel! And I've messed up quite a bit. But the crazy thing about belonging to our Lord is **He makes all things new** (see Revelation 21:5). There is always hope and renewal. We are not stuck in our failures or condemned to a messed-up life because we can't keep our gardens perfectly. In fact, it's impossible for me to catch the little foxes. I really have no power of my own. But the God who defeated the grave . . . well, *He* has all the power I could ever need! And He lives in me. He lives in you too. So if you ever feel like you haven't done that great of a job catching the little foxes and keeping them from trampling your garden, then remember the truth—**God makes all things new.** He gives you a clean slate—every day!—and will work in you to empower you to catch those little foxes and make your garden a place of preparation and beauty.

"Laid Up for You": A Message from the Beloved

> "The mandrakes give forth fragrance,
>   and beside our doors are all choice fruits,
> new as well as old,
>   **which I have laid up for you, O my beloved."**
> (Song of Solomon 7:13; emphasis mine)

There is a second thing you and I are privileged to do: store up every good and pleasing thing for our future husband. It may seem silly to think about preparing your garden for marriage while you're still single or far from marrying age. You might not meet your future hubby until years down the road. You may not have even had a boyfriend yet. Perhaps you've never been kissed. Or perhaps you've been kissed so many times you think "storing up" for your spouse is a lost cause at this point. No. It is not silly, not worthless, to cultivate fruits of goodness and beauty to fill your garden. Even if you were to never marry, those blooming blossoms of purity, service, and gentleness are the very things God wants *all* of His children to possess.

> But the fruit of the Spirit is love, joy, peace, patience, kindness, goodness, faithfulness, gentleness, self-control; against such things there is no law. (Galatians 5:22–23)

So how can you store up such goodness? You must find its root. Look no further than the Gardener. Remember the verse near the beginning of this chapter? Look it up again—Isaiah 61:3: "the planting of the Lord, that He may be glorified." It is He Himself who has masterfully created every stitch of you and has planted inside of you His Holy Spirit. When we talked about character earlier, we found that the Holy Spirit can do some major remodeling within us. He takes the ugliness of our sinful nature and replaces it with the beautiful attributes of Christ Himself. If we are to cultivate a beautiful garden, we must allow the Spirit to dwell there and do His interior-designing work.

So, how do we go about letting the Spirit dwell in us? How do we produce His fruit?

> "I am the true vine, and My Father is the vinedresser. Every branch in Me that does not bear fruit He takes away, and every branch that does bear fruit He prunes, that it may bear more fruit. Already you are clean because of the word that I have spoken to you. Abide in Me, and I in you. As the branch cannot bear fruit by itself, unless it abides in the vine, neither can you, unless you abide in Me." —Jesus (John 15:1–4)

Okay, there's our answer—we have to stay connected to God for the Holy Spirit to do His work. That leads us to the next question: how do we go about staying connected to a God we cannot even see or touch?

Before I answer that, let me ask you a different question. If I were to give you a word for the phrase "a connection between two persons," what word would you think I was talking about? Any guesses?

Relationship

A connection between two persons is a *relationship*. There are many types of relationships—brothers and sisters, wives and husbands, workers and bosses, pastors and congregations—but all of them imply a *connection* between people. When Jesus told us to "abide in the Vine," He was telling us to remain in our connection to Him, to remain in our **relationship** with Him.

How do we cultivate—grow in—our relationship with Christ?

Think about a typical relationship between husband and wife. What is something common in that sort of relationship? Being together, right? Because a husband and wife are bonded together, they want to spend time together. They want to be with the other person, share with the other person, tell the other person about their day, listen to the other person. It is no different with God. He wants to spend time with you. He wants to hear about your day, listen to your problems, share in your joyful moments. He also wants to talk *to* you too. One of the most amazing things in my mind is the fact that God has given us a way to hear Him. When you open His Word, the Bible, He personally comes and speaks directly to you! That's kinda major. This awesome God of the universe has made a way for you to hear Him. And through Christ's sacrifice on the cross, He's made a way for you to talk right to Him. Nothing divides your relationship with God anymore; He's given you intimate access to Himself by tearing the curtain of your sin right in two, from top to bottom (see Mark 15:38).

This access to the presence of God is what keeps our relationship with Him thriving. **To produce the fruits of the Spirit, we must remain connected to Him; to remain connected, we must remain in His Word.** We must daily hear Him by opening His Word and spending time with Him. We must open our own hearts and pour them out by talking to Him. A simple way to start is by doing a morning devotion. Get up a little earlier than you normally would, find a quiet place, put your cell phone in the other room, and open your Bible. A daily devotional book can certainly help you keep a regular reading pattern, or you can read chapters of your own choosing.

I like to start my daily devotions with a journal-entry prayer. I open my spiral-bound notebook and write a letter to God. I tell Him everything—I ask for His mercy where I've failed, I pour out my heart's deepest desires, I lift up others, and I tell Him thank You for all the incredible things He has done. And I ask Him to speak to me. And you know what? He does! I open His Word and read what He has written to me. I'm always surprised at how He can bring me just the right verse, or perhaps a verse that I will need to remember as my day goes by. I always like to end my "morning devo" with a psalm and the Lord's Prayer. Afterward, I know I have sat in the very presence of my God and, because of our time together, I can face whatever my day holds.

.

Remaining together—it's an essential part of staying connected in your relationship with Christ. And it is an essential part in producing the good fruit of the Spirit for your garden. His **living and active Word** accomplishes change inside of you. It has *efficacy* of its own—it's supernatural in its power to fill you with the holiness of the Gardener. And that's how He makes the blossoms grow—His presence inside of you.

> For the word of God is living and active. (Hebrews 4:12a)

How else might you remain connected to Christ?

He has given us an amazing gift in the Sacraments of Holy Baptism and Holy Communion. In Baptism, we experience a physical act in which the Spirit of God becomes a resident within our hearts, and in Holy Communion, we taste and touch the actual body and blood of the Savior whom we cannot see with our eyes. That's pretty remarkable. That's pretty tangible. Our Lord knew that we humans struggle with not being able to touch and see and hear Him. But in these most precious gifts, we are given the chance to indeed reach out and feel Him.

> "This is My body, which is given for you. Do this in remembrance of Me." —Jesus (Luke 22:19b)

By abiding *in* our Savior, we remain in His power to create a beautiful garden within us. A garden with every good delight stored up for our future husband. A garden that speaks of every good wonder of our amazing God.

DELIGHT IN THE ROMANCE OF WAITING

With a garden being cultivated and your heart hoping for "the one," there is joy in waiting for your future husband. I used to see my single life as a burden. *When will he come?!* I was always thinking. I still wonder that, but I'm seeing something beautiful during this time that God has given me to be unmarried. There's much to do!

If I had gotten married when I thought I was ready to be a wife, I would have missed a lot. I was seventeen when I moved away from home to train as an ice dancer. That was the first time I remember being all alone and thinking, *I'm ready to be married.* I wanted someone to share my life with, especially since my family was very far away. I wanted someone to talk to who really *knew* me, inside and out. And I wanted someone to go with me to all these strange and new places I was traveling. I wanted a relationship. Funny thing was, I had one. During those years as a teenager and now as a twenty-something, I had exactly what I needed. Christ was there to share my life; Christ was there to talk to; He knows me inside and out, better than any man ever will. And He has never failed to go with me wherever I have gone. What I couldn't quite see at the time was that I needed to cultivate my relationship with Christ first, **before** I became a wife. I can't imagine the joy I would have missed if I hadn't gotten to know my Lord intimately in the way I have during these single years. He has become my air—my reason for living, my reason to dance, my everything.

And because He has become my everything, I can properly prepare for the season of marriage. Because He has caused me to delight in Him and His way, I'm able to see His design for marriage much more clearly than I did at seventeen (or even a year ago!). Just as we discussed earlier, **falling in love with God is the foundation of all our heart's desires—including marriage.**

So when you find yourself wishing you had a different last name, think about how you might prepare for the day it does change. I'm not just talking about dreaming of your perfect wedding dress, which bridesmaids to ask, or what flavor icing will be on the cake. I'm talking about making yourself ready to be the kind of wife you want to be. Sometimes we think that the moment we put that wedding band on, we'll become some superhero wife and everything will be easy. Ha—yeah; that's not gonna happen! Just as flowers in a garden don't grow the day you put the seed in the soil, so being a godly wife doesn't happen the moment you say "I do." So what can we do in the waiting that will make a difference?

Love him.

Love your future husband right now, today, before you even meet him. We've learned that love is not only feelings; it is a deep commitment and union. You can cultivate those attributes even now. Guard your body and your heart. Memorize Scriptures about marriage. Commit Song of Solomon to memory.

I have a journal—well, two journals—that I keep for my future husband. One has *Ezer Kenegdo* (Hebrew for "sustainer beside him") written on the front of it, and inside I write verses that I want to remember when I am a wife. When I run across Scripture in my devotions that portrays the image of a beautiful union or the godly character of a wife, I write it in the journal. The second journal is full of letters to my future husband. Some have been written on rainy days when my heart was longing to know him. Some have been written from places I've traveled and when  I pondered what it would be like if he were there with me. It's my tangible way of remembering that I can be committed to and love my future husband, whoever he is, even now. And someday, I hope God blesses me with the day he can read them.

You can do other things as well. If you want to be a wife who is a good cook, practice making dinner for your family or friends. If you want to be a wife who is thrifty with her money, practice keeping a budget. If you imagine yourself as a patient mother of three, offer to babysit the neighbor's kids. The possibilities for preparing yourself and your skills are endless. And it can be quite fun to think that you're doing them with serving your future husband in mind. It takes the agony out of waiting and replaces it with anticipation.

Most of all, pray for your future husband.

> The prayer of a righteous person has great power as it is working. (James 5:16b)

God knows who your future spouse is. And you can be sure that when you lift him up in prayer, the Lord hears. Pray that your husband daily seeks God's face. Pray for him to be captivated by God's good design for sex and marriage. Pray that he would be one with you in every aspect of your marriage. And  pray that God will guide you two to each other in HIS timing. When you lay your desire to be a wife, your future husband, and your future marriage at the feet of your Savior, you have put them in the best possible place they can be. And as you wait, rejoice in the fact that God is writing your story, and He always brings you **His best.**

Living in It

In your Bible, read the following Scripture passages and pick verses from each that you want to memorize. Write the verses on a card to put in your pocket and read throughout the day. Perhaps you might even write them in an *Ezer Kenegdo* journal.

Week 9:

- Psalm 45
- 1 Corinthians 6:12–20
- Ephesians 5
- 1 Corinthians 7:4
- 1 Corinthians 10:23–33
- 1 Thessalonians 4:1–12
- Hebrews 13:4
- Genesis 2:18–25
- Genesis 1:27–28
- 1 Peter 3:1–7
- Colossians 1:10–14
- Colossians 3
- Psalm 128

A SPECIAL NOTE FOR YOU
IF YOU'VE LOST YOUR VIRGINITY

Hello, my dear girl,

Was it painful to read through this chapter? Your heart must ache as you consider your own garden and who has come in through the cracks in the wall. Some rose petals have been pulled from the blossoms. Some flower boxes have been walked through—perhaps trampled. The footprints of guilt and hurt have been left behind.

How I long to scoop you up in my arms and take that pain away!

Promise me you'll do one thing. Open your Bible to Romans 8:1–4. Reread verse 1: "There is therefore now **no condemnation** for those who are in Christ Jesus" (Romans 8:1; emphasis mine).

Want to know what Paul had just been talking about right before that? Why the "therefore"? Well, he had just spent chapter 7 agonizing over the battle of his own sin. He felt trapped in a war.

> For I delight in the law of God, in my inner being, but I see in my members another law waging war against the law of my mind and making me captive to the law of sin that dwells in my members. Wretched man that I am! Who will deliver me from this body of death? Thanks be to God through Jesus Christ our Lord! (Romans 7:22–25a)

My dear girl, that is *your* proclamation! Thanks be to God—through Jesus Christ *your* Lord!

Still have doubts? Consider this from the lips of the Lord:

"Come now, let us reason together, says the LORD:
though your sins are like scarlet,
    they shall be as white as snow;
though they are red like crimson,
    they shall become like wool."

(Isaiah 1:18)

Would you like a white wedding dress? Your Father stands ready and waiting to clothe you in the white robe of Christ's righteousness. Let it be yours:

And after six days Jesus took with Him Peter and James and John, and led them up a high mountain by themselves. And He was transfigured before them, and His clothes became radiant, intensely white, as no one on earth could bleach them. (Mark 9:2–3)

For as many of you as were baptized into Christ have put on Christ. (Galatians 3:27)

"But," you exclaim, "under His robe, it's just *me!* I'm still *stained!"*
No. He washed it away. It's gone. You're clean. Wholly clean:

For as high as the heavens are above the earth,
    so great is His steadfast love toward those who fear Him;
as far as the east is from the west,
    so far does He remove our transgressions from us.
As a father shows compassion to His children,
    so the LORD shows compassion to those who fear Him.

(Psalm 103:11–13)

Let me encourage you to reread this Garden chapter. But this time, read it with the knowledge that your Prince has clothed you in splendid white!

With all my love,
Lacy

(Jeremiah 31:33–37)

CHAPTER SIX

Graves and Dry Bones

"Thus says the Lord God: Behold, I will open your graves and raise you from your graves. . . ." (Ezekiel 37:12)

Our personal graves. They come in many different forms, but they all share one thing in common—pain.

> My eye is wasted from grief;
>   my soul and my body also.
> For my life is spent with sorrow,
>   and my years with sighing;
> my strength fails because of my iniquity,
>   and my bones waste away.
>
> (Psalm 31:9b–10)

I had just come from having my heart split open to ache inside my chest—again. I stood there with it gaping, wondering if everyone could see the pain seeping out. Was it written on my face? Or perhaps the people around me were completely oblivious to the fact that something had just died in me. I don't even think he knew . . . which hurt the most. Maybe no one else could see it; certainly no one could touch it; and (hiding my tears until I got in the car), no one heard it. But it was real. The pain was still there.

People may call you overdramatic or too emotional or say you're just going through a "teenage phase" . . . but your pain is real too, huh? I have no doubt that it is. And I have no doubt that by now you've probably felt your own heart split down the middle. Hurts like crazy. It's an ache that seems unreal—as if it doesn't belong in reality. That's why people often discredit it and push it away as nonsense. Don't.

The last thing you want to do with that pain of yours is pretend it isn't real. Convincing yourself that matters of the heart are matters of nonsense discredits the One who made that heart.

> I am feeble and crushed;
>   I groan because of the tumult of my heart.
> O Lord, all my longing is before You;
>   my sighing is not hidden from You.
> My heart throbs; my strength fails me,
>   and the light of my eyes—it also has gone from me.
> (Psalm 38:8–10)

The psalmist David didn't hide his heart from the Lord. He poured out his pain. In fact, many of his psalms may sound rather ridiculous to some. I'm sure there were plenty of people in Israel who wanted to tell him, "Buck up, David! Don't be so dramatic." But God did no such thing. He listened. And He *shared* in David's pain. How can you know? Just look at the tangible example God gave us in His Son on earth. The Lord God sheds tears over our sorrows:

Jesus wept. (John 11:35)

Your sighing and your heartbreak are not hidden from al-mighty God. He sees the depths of your soul's ache. He knows it's real. Doesn't that validate your pain? Isn't it reassuring to know that you're not crazy for hurting this badly? I don't think you're crazy, and the Lord doesn't think you're crazy—He endured this *very pain of yours* on the cross that day on Calvary. You are not the only one who has carried it. He bore it too. He shared in it.

> You have seen my affliction;
> You have known the distress of my soul.
> (Psalm 31:7b)

Our pains and heartbreaks have been fully KNOWN. Isn't that what we all really long for? There are times when we don't want someone else to fix it. We don't want to be given advice about how to get over it or how to get back on our feet. Sometimes we just want our pain to be known. We want someone to touch—even just a little bit—our ache inside and understand just how deep it is. Just how penetrating and consuming it is. Just how sad our heart feels. No need to fix it; we only want someone to *share* in it.

That's one thing Job's friends did right when they came to vis-it him (Job 2:11–13). Eventually, they offered all sorts of advice and well-intended opinions to the guy who had just lost everything, but for the first seven days, they simply sat on the ground with Job and said nothing. Seven days! Can you imagine how tired their back-sides were from sitting on the hard ground for a week? But they were there. They were present. They were alongside him, sharing in his pain. And that was what Job needed in that moment.

Is that what you need too? Someone to agree with you that your pain is real? Someone who understands it even if no one else does . . . even if you don't fully understand it yourself? That's what I find myself longing for when my heart splits in two. I'll take a bandage later, but for now, just someone please acknowledge that what I feel is real!

Mary and Martha had that Someone: Jesus. You see, their beloved brother, Lazarus, had just died. They had sent word to Jesus that he was sick—and Jesus was only a short day's walk away. But Jesus stayed where He was for two days after He got the news. Jesus knew that Lazarus had to die and had to lie in his grave. There was a purpose in that. So He waited.

On the fourth day after Lazarus's death, Jesus went to Bethany, to the home of Mary and Martha. Their hearts were broken, and Jesus knew just how to touch each woman's grief.

Martha ran out and exclaimed, "If You had been here, my brother would not have died" (John 11:21). Jesus knew Martha well. She had been the one who had rushed around in a frenzy, making all sorts of preparations for Jesus' visit, while her sister, Mary, simply sat at Jesus' feet and listened (Luke 10:40). Jesus knew that Martha was a woman who got things done. She needed explanations and details and plans and answers; she needed things to be mapped out nice and logical so she could analyze them. Jesus understood that. And so He responded:

> "Your brother will rise again. . . . I am the resurrection and the life. Whoever believes in Me, though he die, yet shall he live, and everyone who lives and believes in Me will never die. Do you believe this?" (John 11:23, 25–26)

She did. She did believe it. And that's what she needed—her Savior's voice offering truth and a tangible reminder of faith for her to hold onto. He pointed her to Himself and His power, creating a sturdy hope for her to wrap herself around. She needed her Lord to know her pain and speak to it in just the right way.

Her sister, Mary, needed something else. She also ran out to meet Jesus: "Lord, if You had been here, my brother would not have died" (John 11:32). Jesus knew Mary well too. She had been the one sitting at His feet, listening to every word He said (Luke 10:39). And He knew she would later be the woman who anointed Him for His own death by pouring a pint of expensive perfume on His feet and wiping it up with the locks of her hair (John 12:3). She wasn't as concerned about explanations, details, and answers. She was quiet, gentle, and tender in her words and spirit. And Jesus knew just how to speak to her pain:

> When Jesus saw her weeping, . . . He was deeply moved in His spirit and greatly troubled. . . . Jesus wept. (John 11:33, 35)

After He had touched each woman's pain, He spoke newness into life. With three words—"Lazarus, come out" (John 11:43)—Jesus raised the hopes of Mary and Martha.

I love Jesus' response to Martha right before He raised Lazarus from the tomb:

> Jesus said, "Take away the stone." Martha, the sister of the dead man, said to Him, "Lord, by this time there will be an odor, for he has been dead four days." Jesus said to her, "Did I not tell you that if you believed, you would see the glory of God?" (John 11:39–40)

Oh, logical Martha. I'm a lot like her sometimes. And I'm a lot like Mary sometimes too. I think we all are a combination of the two. But Jesus' answer to us, and to all, is the same as it was to Martha: *"Did I not tell you that if you believed, you would see the glory of God?"* Isn't that the ultimate reason for all our pain—so that in that fragile place, we can surrender to simple trust and thus know the rolling away of the stone by Christ to reveal the glory of God?

> "This illness [Lazarus's] does not lead to death. It is for the glory of God, so that the Son of God may be glorified through it." (John 11:4)

Even before He came and comforted the sisters and raised the dead brother from the grave, Jesus knew *exactly* what this trial and pain would produce. It was for something incredible. It had a purpose—a divine purpose.

Sometimes that is so very hard for us to see. We sit waiting in our grief; we've sent word to the Healer; He's surely not that far away! And **yet,** He waits.

> Now Jesus **loved** Martha and her sister and Lazarus. **So,** when He heard that Lazarus was ill, He stayed two days longer in the place where He was. (John 11:5–6; emphasis mine)

Does it mean He doesn't love us when He stays where He is? We wonder that, don't we? It seems that if He truly cared about us, He would rush to our side and stop the pain. Or arrive in time to prevent the pain and stop what could cause it. He could have kept Lazarus from dying. Even the Jews who came from Jerusalem knew that: "Could not He who opened the eyes of the blind man also have kept this man from dying?" (John 11:37). Of course He could have! But He knew that Lazarus needed to lie in that grave. There was something important about letting him go there.

There is something important about letting us go there too. Our heartbreak-graves are not fun places; they are filled with our grief, devastating pain, and sheer brokenness. They feel as much a place of death as we have ever felt before. But there *is* something important about them.

When we are in that place where we can do nothing about our pain—nothing to heal it, nothing to lessen it, nothing to stop it or reverse it or even just make it an ounce better—that is when we have truly become like dry bones within our graves. Take it from the prophet Ezekiel:

> The hand of the LORD was upon me, and He brought me out in the Spirit of the LORD and set me down in the middle of the

valley; it was full of bones. And He led me around among them, and behold, there were very many on the surface of the valley, and behold, they were very dry. And He said to me, "Son of man, can these bones live?" And I answered, "O Lord God, You know." (Ezekiel 37:1–3)

Dry bones can do nothing about their situation. Isn't it the same for us? The grave is a place where we can take no action on our own. That is exactly where my heartache often puts me. I often wonder why my Lord would ever let me reach the point where my hurts are that paralyzing and crushing. But He lets me reach that point so I will know that **He** is the one who breathes me back to life:

Then He said to me, "Prophesy over these bones, and say to them, O dry bones, hear the word of the LORD. Thus says the Lord God to these bones: Behold, I will cause breath to enter you, and you shall live. And I will lay sinews upon you, and will cause flesh to come upon you, and cover you with skin, and put breath in you, and you shall live, and you shall know that I am the LORD."

So I prophesied as I was commanded. And as I prophesied, there was a sound, and behold, a rattling, and the bones came together, bone to its bone. And I looked, and behold, there were sinews on them, and flesh had come upon them, and skin had covered them. But there was no breath in them. Then He said to me, "Prophesy to the breath; prophesy, son of man, and say to the breath, Thus says the Lord God: Come from the four winds, O breath, and breathe on these slain, that they may live." So I prophesied as He commanded me, and the breath came into them, and they lived and stood on their feet, an exceedingly great army. (Ezekiel 37:4–10)

The Lord had asked Ezekiel, "Can these bones live?"
The Lord had asked Martha, "Do you believe this?"

And now, the Lord asks you. You, who are lying as dry bones in your grave of pain. You, who sent word for Him to come. You, who exclaimed, "Lord, if you had been here . . ."

Hear Him as He comes to touch your pain, as only He can do:

> "Son of man, these bones are the whole house of Israel. Behold, they say, 'Our bones are dried up, and our hope is lost; we are indeed cut off.' Therefore prophesy, and say to them, Thus says the Lord God: Behold, I will open your graves and raise you from your graves, O my people. And I will bring you into the land of Israel." (Ezekiel 37:11–12)

The grave. He's let you lie in it.

His grave. It's empty.

Your dry bones. He has five words for them:

> "Take off the grave clothes."—Jesus (John 11:44b [NIV])

"THEN YOU, MY PEOPLE, WILL KNOW . . ."

> "And you shall know that I am the LORD, when I open your graves, and raise you from your graves, O My people. And I will put My Spirit within you, and you shall live, and I will place you in your own land. Then you shall know that I am the LORD; I have spoken, *and I will do it,* declares the LORD." (Ezekiel 37:13–14, emphasis mine)

Our graves provide the place where our pain can be shared. Where our pain can be fully **known.** For He, too, lay in one after feeling in His own body on the cross the very pain that you struggle with right now. Our graves also provide the place where our pain produces something for us to **know**—that only the resurrected Lord could ever give us life.

> Jesus said to her, "I am the resurrection and the life. Whoever believes in Me, though he die, yet shall he live, and everyone who lives and believes in Me shall never die. Do you believe this?" (John 11:25–26)

Only two words are needed, and He is the one who will give you the breath to say them:

> "Yes, Lord." (John 11:27a)

What's more, not only will you know, but the people who witness Him raising you out of despair will know too:

> Many of the Jews therefore, who had come with Mary and had seen what He did, believed in Him. (John 11:45)

Who could have imagined that our graves of pain and heartbreak could hold treasures of faith and life—for ourselves and for the world? Purposeful? I'd say so. Beautiful? Not a doubt. If the reason for our pain is for His glory, then how beautiful a plan our pain can bring about! The Lord used Lazarus's death to show Christ's ability—His power over death—and His love. But to do that, a grave had to exist. He used it to touch Mary and Martha's hearts in just the right way; to show He was that kind of Savior; to bring faith to the Jews visiting them; to show His disciples that death was no match for Him; and to breathe new life into a man who was well on his way to becoming a pile of dry bones. Imagine Lazarus's life after that fateful day! Do you think he had something to tell everyone? You betcha! I imagine he couldn't keep his mouth shut about the kind Savior who chose to use *His* grave as a way to illuminate God's glory.

And that's what He wants for you too. He wants to share in your hurt, to tell you that it is real, to feel it with you . . . and then raise you from it! He will not leave you dead and dry as a valley of bones. No! No matter what "little deaths" come your way, He will be the resurrection and life that lifts you from them and heals your hurting heart in the process.

Feel like you can't pull yourself from your heartache? Good. He can. And He *will*. He's asking you to trust Him.

"Yes, Lord."

Big Ol' Zero

If the cross is the "big ol' *X*" God uses to strike out our sin and our brokenness, then the empty grave is the "big ol' zero" that cancels them all out. Multiply your pain against the empty grave's value and what is the sum? Take any digit of trial, heartbreak, or horrible thing that has happened and put it up against the Easter grave and what do you get? (Math isn't my best subject, but I know this multiplication principle!) $156{,}237 \times 0 = \mathbf{0}$!

Doesn't it seem that everything else in life just adds to your pain?

- Your heart bleeds from being rejected, then you see your ex with his new girl—multiply pain by ten.
- Your parents sign the divorce papers, then you sit in the car, traveling to Dad's for the weekend— multiply by twenty-seven.
- You invest in your best friend's life, then she betrays you—multiply by thirteen.

Sometimes, it seems that it never stops. So much around us not only reminds us of our broken hearts, it increases the hurt.

Remember when I said that our graves are the place where **we** can't do anything to lessen our pain? **Well, when nothing in this life can subtract from the hurt, the empty tomb can.**

I began this chapter by telling you that I had just experienced my own heart splitting open again. I finish this chapter after several days have gone by. They were hard days. Very hard days—complete with migraine and red, puffy eyes. I really did feel like no one fully understood what I was feeling or why I felt the way I did. And I felt that everyone thought it wasn't something to be heartbroken over. But most of all, I felt like I could do NOTHING to lessen the hurt, and that hurt wouldn't leave me alone. It clung to me all through my day and into my night. I couldn't even imagine how the Lord was going to make it any better—that's how penetrating it was. But the Lord Jesus knew just how He needed to touch it, even if I didn't.

He had let the grave come, but He didn't leave me in it alone. He stood by me and wept with me because that's what my heart needed. He spread the warmth of healing over me and started to bind up my broken heart (Isaiah 61:1).

How?

Well, it wasn't a change in my circumstances. It was just His presence. The presence of One who would cry with me—of One who knew all of me and knew all of my pain. The presence of true Life and Resurrection.

When you stand in what feels like death, having Life right beside you changes something. When you have no hope left, having the very embodiment of Hope Made Flesh standing with you does something. When you have no power to move your dry bones, having the almighty Breath of Life holding your hand creates something. When you sit in an enclosure of darkness, having the Light of the World alongside you changes the scenery. When you lie in your grave, having the risen Jesus call your name brings you back to life.

Your circumstances may not change and you may feel helpless in your hurt, but that doesn't mean that God cannot create something new. That is the message and the reality of the empty tomb of Easter. Whatever may come, it has been conquered. Whatever brings death, it is no match for the risen Savior. When pain vacuums the air from your lungs, He will breathe life into you anew. No matter how many times your heart breaks, remember—**He makes all things new!**

> I will extol You, O LORD, for You have drawn me up
>   and have not let my foes rejoice over me.
> O LORD my God, I cried to You for help,
>   and You have healed me.
> O LORD, You have brought up my soul from Sheol;
>   You restored me to life from among those who go
>   down to the pit. . . .
>
> You have turned for me my mourning into dancing;
>   You have loosed my sackcloth
>   and clothed me with gladness,
> that my glory may sing Your praise and not be silent.
>   O LORD my God, I will give thanks to You forever!
> (Psalm 30:1–3, 11–12)

▪

> He who was seated on the throne said, "Behold, I am
>   making all things new." (Revelation 21:5a)

Pocket It

The promises of God found in His Word can resuscitate the dry bones of any grave. Look up these passages in your Bible, and after you've read them, mark the verses that speak to your heart. Then, write them on a piece of paper to place in your pocket or purse.

Week 10:

- Psalm 31
- Isaiah 61
- Psalm 34
- Zephaniah 3:14–20
- Lamentations 3

Conclusion

I Pulled One Lace Tight . . .

Why was I going forward with this today? I had just been in a car accident, and I still felt the radiating vibrations of shock throughout my body. But I knew exactly what I was doing. I was going to tell everyone what He just did. This is what I wanted—what I was made to do. *This* was my dream. "What has God done?" echoed against the walls of my brain. I stepped onto the smooth white sheet of ice—where every ounce of my being longed to be.

The day before, I had written in my journal:

> **Saturday, December 15, 2012**
>
> I'm nervous, Father, about tomorrow. I want to skate my best—but most of all, I want to live in each moment as in a prayer, as in a Scripture verse, as in a moment face-to-face with You.
>
> And tomorrow I want everyone to see Your Son and the Father whose love came through Him.
>
> Help me to show the audience that You are jealous for me.
>
> O Father, please send Your angels to lift me up in Your arms so that I might glide for You and portray Your grace. O Lord God—I can't believe *this* is what You've given me to do! It makes my heart soar! Thank You!!!

My heavenly Father soon took my request and made it more real than I ever could have imagined. As my car slid around the icy corner, I felt the tires slipping out of control. My car veered into the other lane and then came back around—and I knew that I had lost it. Out went a panicked cry for help. My Father heard. Little did I know, He was already answering.

I looked at my hands still gripping the steering wheel. Why weren't they bleeding? Why wasn't I upside down? I was sure the embankment would have tossed my little car on its roof. But there it sat—upright on the wheels. The cloud of airbag dust made the cabin feel small and eerie, and the items thrown from their places resembled the thoughts inside my brain.

Then someone was there. "Miss, are you all right?"

I was. I was more than all right.

As I left the scene of the crash, my car mangled in snowy wreckage, I had a very strange peace. The sickening panic I expected to feel in my stomach was instead a glassy calm. Something incredible had just happened: I knew that God had saved me to skate that night.

I was praying the ER doctor agreed. The nurses were skeptical: "You can't skate today! You were just in an accident!"

Yes, yes that was true. "But you don't understand," I wanted to say as I choked back tears (so as not to ruin my ice-show makeup). "My Lord saved me so I could skate tonight! I've planned on telling the world what He has done through my skating program . . . and now I have every reason to!"

When the nurses walked out to get the doctor and left me all alone, I stared down at my body in the hospital gown. My throat tightened with the repressed tears. "O Lord, *please*, let me skate tonight! *Please!* My message about You is why this happened!"

Had not the angels I prayed for lifted me up? They had lifted me in my car and placed me safely on the other side of an embankment. No broken bones. No bloody hands. Not even a wound from the shards of windshield glass. Just one little scratch on my knee as a potent reminder of my mortality. The mortality I now knew I needed to use to proclaim a gift of eternal immortality that I had been given.

The doctor cleared me. "I hear you have a skating show to get to." He told me I'd feel like a semi-truck had run me over tomorrow, but today I could skate. A hospital gown has never come off so quickly!

Later, at the rink, I couldn't get my skates on and laced quickly enough. There was something I had to say, and I knew I would never be able to express it fully off the ice. I had choreographed the beginning sequence to be solemn, but I couldn't help smiling. The soft proclamation of the lyrics were the *very* words of my own heart— they spoke of His compassion for me!

I have never felt as I did that night on the ice. **That** is why I was created. There were no thoughts to technique or positions or perfect toe point . . . there was only me and my Lord. It had never been that way before. Oh, I had felt God smiling as I skated in the past, but this time there was no program or routine as there had been before. This time, it was me actually living every word of the song.

It was a prayer in motion.

This was the moment I stood face-to-face with my Father—crying with joy as I was washed over by the flood of His real grace toward me. I knew being the moving picture of His grace on the ice was now His gift to me. And suddenly I also knew the gift of true worship had been given to me—as I acknowledged that **He came to me** to offer all He had done. The tears fell as the music played. I was living my heart. I was dancing my heart.

The pieces of my past all at once seemed to make sense as my blades pushed through the white ice. The years I spent searching for an ice-dance partner; the many times I moved all alone to yet another part of the country; the eating disorder; the mental abuse; walking out of the ice-show contract; coming home with nothing left but remnants of a dream. It all made sense. Even the heartache and mistakes from my past relationships and the horror of my parents' divorce—it all had a place.

"As for you, you meant evil against me, but God meant it for good, to bring it about that many people should be kept alive, as they are today." —Joseph (Genesis 50:20)

My Lord took a road that was broken and filled with wreckage and He made it the ingredients that composed something beautiful.

"So shall My word be that goes out from My mouth;
    it shall not return to Me empty,
but it shall accomplish that which I purpose,
    and shall succeed in the thing for which I sent it.

"For you shall go out in joy
    and be led forth in peace;
the mountains and the hills before you
    shall break forth into singing,
    and all the trees of the field shall clap their hands.
Instead of the thorn shall come up the cypress;
    instead of the brier shall come up the myrtle;
and it shall make a name for the Lord,
    an everlasting sign that shall not be cut off."

(Isaiah 55:11–13)

I continually thank God for that car crash. If ever there was a moment when I glimpsed divine clarity, it was that day. It wasn't just that He saved me; it was that He **had** saved me. And because of the rescue He provided for my soul, everything else had meaning. Everything else had a place and a purpose. And everything else was a channel funneling His love and compassion directly to me in ways that brought only good. He had taken the darkest nights of my journey and molded them into the puzzle pieces I needed to see the redeemed picture of my life. What other god could do such a thing? What other god could take the personal horrors I

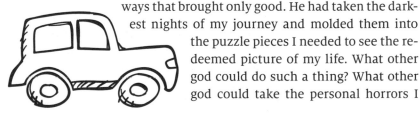

had known and use them *again and again* to provide for me the desires of my heart?

He has taught me that because I am His, what looks like disaster is **always** . . . not.

> For My thoughts are not your thoughts,
>> neither are your ways My ways, declares the Lord.
>
> (Isaiah 55:8)

And no matter what comes my way on this earthly journey, He will be faithful to always bring me good.

> "For the mountains may depart
>> and the hills be removed,
>
> but My steadfast love shall not depart from you,
>> and My covenant of peace be removed,"
>> says the Lord, who has compassion on you.

> "O afflicted one, storm-tossed and not comforted,
>> behold, I will set your stones in antimony,
>> and lay your foundations with sapphires.
>
> I will make your pinnacles of agate,
>> your gates of carbuncles,
>> and all your wall of precious stones. . . .

> "In righteousness you shall be established;
>> you shall be far from oppression, for you shall not fear;
>> and from terror, for it shall not come near you.
>
> If anyone stirs up strife,
>> it is not from Me;
>
> whoever stirs up strife with you
>> shall fall because of you.
>
> Behold, I have created the smith
>> who blows the fire of coals
>> and produces a weapon for its purpose.
>
> I have also created the ravager to destroy;
>> no weapon that is fashioned against you shall succeed,

and you shall refute every tongue that rises against
    you in judgment.
This is the heritage of the servants of the LORD
    and their vindication from Me, declares the LORD."
(Isaiah 54:10–12, 14–17)

It still seems incomprehensible—**nothing** can overcome His love for me. "Nor height nor depth, nor anything else in all creation, will be able to separate us from the love of God in Christ Jesus our Lord" (Romans 8:39). Nothing can overcome His love *for you.*

It may feel at times that the darkness has won. But it hasn't. It may feel like everything you loved has been stripped away. But it isn't. It may feel like the road you've walked cannot become beautiful. But it is. Look not to what the pieces of your life appear to be, but instead let Him show you what He uses them to be. And when you think how incomprehensible it is that He is doing everything for your benefit, may your heart truly say:

But as for me, the nearness of God is my good.
(Psalm 73:28a [NASB])

THE ANSWER

I remember thinking as a young girl, *Why don't Christians ever deal with problems in a real way? All they talk about is the cross, the cross, the cross!*

Oh boy, did I ever have a lot to learn about . . . well, about everything. I thought the "solution" of the cross was a cop-out. How could the cross really solve every problem, answer every question, be the medicine for every disease and the bandage for every wound? I wasn't ready to believe that this one moment in history could address every other moment in history. Weren't there more meaningful solutions to be had, other ways that faith could make a difference?

And weren't there other parts of Scripture that were more suited to the problems we all face?

Uh. . . . No.

The message of the cross had become just a familiar story. I had heard the Good Friday and Easter Sunday readings so many times that I stopped listening. Throw out a quick John 3:16, and there ya have it—salvation! Now time to move on to more pressing matters. Like broken hearts, broken dreams, broken families, depression, fear, betrayal. I couldn't see how the cross was relevant to any of that.

I was so wrong. I couldn't have been more wrong.

I wonder what God's face looked like when I was thinking those things as a young girl. I don't think He scowled. I think He perhaps thought ahead to December 16, 2012, and smiled. He wouldn't give up on me.

WITHOUT THE CROSS

Have you ever wondered what life would be like without the cross? I have.

Without the cross, He wouldn't work everything for our good. We'd still be His enemies. And we would feel His wrath eternally.

> A fearful expectation of judgment, and a fury of fire . . . will consume the adversaries [of God]. (Hebrews 10:27)

Without the cross, we couldn't approach Him. The curtain would still divide His holiness from our stain-fulness.

> "You cannot see My face, for man shall not see Me and live." — God (Exodus 33:20)

Without the cross, we couldn't please Him. Isn't that what every child longs to do—please her parent? "Look what I did, Daddy!" "Watch me, Mommy!" Before the cross, it wasn't a possibility.

> We have all become like one who is unclean,
>> and all our righteous deeds are like **a polluted garment.**
> We all fade like a leaf,
>> and our iniquities, like the wind, take us away.
>
> (Isaiah 64:6; emphasis mine)

■

> Those who are in the flesh cannot please God. (Romans 8:8)

Without the cross, everything in life would be meaningless— an empty span of purposeless years that gnaw away at your broken heart.

> So I [Solomon] hated life, because what is done under the sun was grievous to me, for all is vanity and a striving after wind. (Ecclesiastes 2:17)

Without the cross, this earthly life would be all there is to hope in . . . and as we've seen, that isn't much hope at all.

> But he who is joined with all the living has hope, for a living dog is better than a dead lion. For the living know that they will die, but the dead know nothing, and they have no more reward, for the memory of them is forgotten. Their love and their hate and their envy have already perished, and forever they have no more share in all that is done under the sun. (Ecclesiastes 9:4–6)

Finding fulfilling love—not a chance. Living out a beautiful covenant of marriage—nope. Getting up each morning in joyful expectation—you're dreaming! Consider what your life would be like had

His cross never existed . . . Not the prettiest picture, is it? I would have a hard time just breathing in and out under that load of darkness.

WITH THE CROSS

But life with the cross? Is it really any different?

Let's see:

With the cross, our God brings us **perfect love.** It is a love that does something incredible to our fear.

> There is no fear in love, but perfect love casts out fear. For fear has to do with punishment. (1 John 4:18a)

With the cross, God the Son invites us to come to Him. No more division. No more hiding His face. No more curtain.

> We have this as a sure and steadfast anchor of the soul, a hope that enters into the inner place behind the curtain, where Jesus has gone as a forerunner on our behalf. (Hebrews 6:19–20a)

With the cross, we can make Him smile. He bestows upon us the power and ability to do what brings Him pleasure.

> Through Him then let us continually offer up a sacrifice of praise to God, that is, the fruit of lips that acknowledge His name. Do not neglect to do good and to share what you have, for such sacrifices are pleasing to God. (Hebrews 13:15–16)

With the cross, what once was a cavern of void and meaningless days is now a treasure of fulfilling purpose awaiting our cultivation.

> Whatever you do, work heartily, as for the Lord and not for men, knowing that from the Lord you will receive the inheritance as your reward. You are serving the Lord Christ. (Colossians 3:23–24)

With the cross, we have hope and **assurance** of a perfect life in heaven. Broken lists of life are gone!

> Blessed be the God and Father of our Lord Jesus Christ! According to His great mercy, He has caused us to be born again to a living hope through the resurrection of Jesus Christ from the dead, to an inheritance that is imperishable, undefiled, and unfading, kept in heaven for you. (1 Peter 1:3–4)

Pretty big difference, isn't it? How can two crossbeams reverse the most horrible facts of our existence? By holding up a God who clothed Himself in weak and beaten flesh. By holding up a God who knew you could never see His face in paradise because you were too dirty. By holding up a God who could have held up the whole world with His pinky finger, but decided to put aside that power so He could be like you and me. By holding up a God who wanted to walk with you—not just look down upon you. By holding up a God who died.

A God who died. Isn't that remarkable? Sending someone who could "take care of business" on behalf of almighty God . . . sure, we could see that. Send the CEO or company manager, completely abandoning the creation and people He made . . . sure, what are we compared to Him? We'd turned our back on Him anyhow. But an immortal God who willingly chose to become one of us and to be vulnerable to an unjust and horrifying death—to save the people who nailed Him up there?

Wow. If any single event in history could change every other event in history, that would be it.

And it was. The cross isn't just for the one day of your salvation—**it's for every day of your life.** If you can't find the answer to your question (no matter what your question is), look there. Want to understand why you were born and what you should do with your tomorrows? Look there. Do you find yourself in need—of money, direction, love, healing? Look there.

It is the most beautiful place, that spot at the Savior's feet. The world may be rushing around you, chasing after every need, pleasure, or plan—but that home near your Savior's feet provides everything you need for everything needed. The cross is no empty copout. It is **The Answer.** It is the reason to live and the provision of our heart's desire. It is what the Old Testament pointed forward to and the New Testament points back to. And it is the very moment that every aspect of your life is tied to.

■

I was wrong in thinking the cross couldn't address the pressing matters of broken hearts, broken dreams, fear, hurt, and unrequited love. The reality of life on this earth is that all those matters continue to exist even after a person is saved. But those matters were given a closing chapter with the words uttered from the cross, "**It is finished**" (John 19:30). Their power to hold us in chains of fear and darkness has been obliterated.

But how do we know for sure?

The tomb.

Hollow and missing the Person who was supposed to be rotting away inside. If the stone had been rolled back to expose the decay of Jesus of Nazareth's body . . . well, I'd have to find another source to put my hope in, for hope cannot be placed in something or someone dead.

> God raised Him up, loosing the pangs of death, because it was not possible for Him to be held by it. For David says concerning Him,
>
> "I saw the Lord always before me,
>   for He is at my right hand that I may not be shaken;
> therefore my heart was glad, and my tongue rejoiced;
>   my flesh also will dwell in hope.

> For You will not abandon my soul to Hades,
>   or let Your Holy One see corruption.
> You have made known to me the paths of life;
>   You will make me full of gladness with Your presence."
>
> (Acts 2:25–28)

Not only did He provide the answer, He provided the assurance that it was true. When you gaze at the Easter tomb, let your heart rest assured that if death could be defeated on your behalf, then all others things have been defeated as well.

■

My dear girl, your life in this rather crazy, messy, confusing world is a life that has been **redeemed.** The bad parts—conquered. The dark nights of the soul—interrupted by glorious light. The struggles of your body—touched by a Healer. The reflection in the mirror—more beautiful to Him than life. Hidden secrets of shame— robed in dazzling white. Bleeding hearts—bound by perfect love. Fragile hopes—held by your Father. Your story—written to work all for your good. Your future—brimming with His faithfulness.

Your life—*His.*

And that, my girl, is the reason to live.
I pray it will be the reason you live.

As You Go On

Much will come at you during these years of your life. The neon signs will be aglow brighter than they have ever been before. Flashing arrows will point in directions that everyone seems to be walking, and the interior designer of worldly character will try ever so hard to peddle his counterfeit plastics at your door. When it seems the messages are inescapable, remember that you have been equipped with one far greater. You have been given Truth.

> Stand therefore, having fastened on the belt of truth, and having put on the breastplate of righteousness, and, as shoes for your feet, having put on the readiness given by the gospel of peace. In all circumstances take up the shield of faith, with which you can extinguish all the flaming darts of the evil one; and take the helmet of salvation, and the sword of the Spirit, which is the word of God, praying at all times in the Spirit, with all prayer and supplications. (Ephesians 6:14–18a)

And as Paul prayed for the Church in Ephesus, so I pray for you today and always, my dear girl:

> I do not cease to give thanks for you, remembering you in my prayers, that the God of our Lord Jesus Christ, the Father of glory, may give you the Spirit of wisdom and of revelation in the knowledge of Him, having the eyes of your hearts enlightened, that you may know what is the hope to which He has called you, what are the riches of His glorious inheritance in the saints, and what is the immeasurable greatness of His power toward us who believe, according to the working of His great might that He worked in Christ when He raised Him from the dead and seated Him at His right hand in the heavenly places, far above all rule and authority and power and dominion, and above every name that is named, not only in this age but also in the one to come. And He put all things under His feet and gave Him as head over all things to the church, which is His body, the fullness of Him who fills all in all. (Ephesians 1:16–23)

· ■ ·

As you come to the last pages of this book and continue on with your story, and perhaps take a little of mine with you, remember the God who writes them both. Remember the God who grants complete victory at that muddy spot near His feet. Remember the God who created a place for you to belong in His own body. The God who knows you are worth the sacrifice of His human life. The God who cancels out your shame and breaks your most fear-filled chains. Remember the God who couldn't live without you and will faithfully and mysteriously turn your days of disaster into bountiful blessings to benefit you. Remember the God who breathed life into your bones and reached to grab you from your dark pit. The God who planted talents and dreams and desires inside your heart and made your feet beautiful. Remember the God who gives you purpose to get up every morning and to sleep soundly every night. Remember the God who answered your every question with the reality of a cross and empty tomb. Remember the God who picked you. Remember the God who is your Lover Eternal. Remember the God who *remembers* you.

And I pray you will live every day of your life captivated by this Lord who has made you His own.

> Blessed is he whose help is the God of Jacob,
>   whose hope is in the LORD his God,
> who made heaven and earth,
>   the sea, and all that is in them,
> who keeps faith forever.
>
> (Psalm 146:5–6)

■

Watch out crazy, messy,
confusing world—
a Godly and girly girl is
ready to shine His light!

✳